GATHER AT THE TABLE

GATHER AT THE TABLE

*The Healing Journey of a
Daughter of Slavery and
a Son of the Slave Trade*

Thomas Norman DeWolf
and Sharon Leslie Morgan

Foreword by Joy Angela DeGruy, PhD,
author of *Post Traumatic Slave Syndrome*

BEACON PRESS
BOSTON

Beacon Press
Boston, Massachusetts
www.beacon.org

Beacon Press books
are published under the auspices of
the Unitarian Universalist Association of Congregations.

20 19 18 17   8 7 6 5 4 3 2

This book is printed on acid-free paper that meets the uncoated paper
ANSI/NISO specifications for permanence as revised in 1992.

Text design and composition by Wilsted & Taylor Publishing Services

Library of Congress Cataloging-in-Publication Data
DeWolf, Thomas Norman
Gather at the table : the healing journey of a daughter
of slavery and a son of the slave trade / Thomas Norman DeWolf and
Sharon Leslie Morgan ; foreword by Joy Angela DeGruy.
p. cm.
Includes bibliographical references.
ISBN 978-0-8070-1444-8 (paperback: alk. paper)
1. Slavery—United States—History. 2. United States—Race relations.
I. Morgan, Sharon Leslie. II. Title.
E441.D49 2012
306.3'620973—dc23   2012009318

For our ancestors who guide us

For our children who inspire us

For our grandchildren
who keep our hopes alive

CONTENTS

FOREWORD

The Akan people of Ghana, in West Africa, have long used Adinkra symbols to communicate important philosophical ideas and beliefs. The Sankofa icon is a mythical bird flying forward but looking backward. In its mouth is an egg. The image embodies a dual meaning. The egg represents knowledge of the past, on which wisdom is based, and signifies as well the benefit of that wisdom to future generations. The Sankofa urges us to "go back and get it."

This is precisely what Thomas Norman DeWolf (a white man who is the descendant of traders and owners of enslaved Africans) and Sharon Leslie Morgan (a black woman who is the descendant of enslaved Africans) committed themselves to doing. Over the course of an epic journey, they physically traveled thousands of miles. Emotionally, they traversed oceans and centuries.

Gather at the Table is the experience of two unique and courageous individuals, seen through their particular lenses and shared from their distinct vantage points. Using genealogical records, historical references, and gut instincts, they ventured to places, thoughts, and emotions few of us would be willing to explore or experience. Inspired by a healing model, they sought to understand their history and to try and make sense of it. Their end goal was to make the connections necessary to healing themselves and, they ultimately hoped, others from the intractable wounds caused by slavery, racism, and the traumas of oppression.

In writing about their journey, they neatly weave their individual perspectives of events and experiences; these are sometimes in such sharp contrast that it is difficult to believe they were in the same place at the same time. But this is the stuff of real life; the nitty-gritty that both dia-metrically separates us and brings us together as human beings. Neither Tom nor Sharon shies away from the tough moments when emotions run high and opinions clash. They both recognize that the terrain is rough and not suited for the faint of heart. This is no fairytale. There are no magical remedies or mythical characters that rush forth to save the day. Like any good story, there is adventure and excitement, juxtaposed against amazing moments of personal realization and clarity.

For Sharon, race is a "real" place where she has lived her whole life. At times, she is overcome with grief and anger: *"Stolen land! Stolen people! Murder! If there is a God and he condones retribution, the white race owes a sh*tload!"* Yet it was a white man—Lawson Mabry, with whom Sharon had only corresponded about her genealogy work—who, in her words, "offered emotional solace to an angry black woman who needed answers."

For Tom, race is a place he has only recently *chosen* to visit. Still, he was undaunted by the unknown and sometimes frightening and racially charged alleyways he would venture down. He experiences strong emo-tions that are equally intense: "What has come as a surprise is that I feel more pessimistic than when we began. I recognize more than ever just how deeply embedded systems of oppression remain." Unwilling to give in to futility, Tom shares, "What gives me hope are individual relation-ships. I don't care so much about laws changing if people's hearts aren't going to change."

Together, Tom and Sharon allow us to be spectators of their story— witnesses to their discomfort, humiliation, and fear—in order to educate us and thus contribute to healing a nation in the throes of racial upheaval.

Theirs was an endeavor I found myself envying. I imagined walking in the footsteps of my own ancestors, learning about their lives, seeing the environments in which they lived, toiled, laughed, and cried. What would it have been like to travel with Tom and Sharon, I wondered, to be on a plantation and sleep in the "Big House"; to hear the stories, true and untrue, about the lives of the enslaved and enslavers; and to compare these stories with what they knew and had studied?

This is a true story about two people who defied the odds and shattered the myth that unity between black and white is not possible. Tom and Sharon offer a gift to posterity with this rich recounting of their personal histories, as well as an important piece of America's history told through the eyes of two of slavery's children. They offer hope and encouragement to all of us who aspire to engage in a process of "change"—to right the wrongs of the past and forge a more just and peaceful future.

Although their journey was fraught with hardship and complexity, Tom and Sharon conclude that, in the end, it was all worth it: "We began as two disconnected people. We learned. We argued. We struggled. We grew. We laughed. We cried. We changed. Along the way, we became friends."

JOY ANGELA DEGRUY, PHD
author of *Post Traumatic Slave Syndrome*

INTRODUCTION

Sharon's Story

"F**k that dumbass Obama!"

I live in a small town in a rural community in the Northeast; a working-class town of 1,230 people, predominately white. My arrival in 2010 increased the black population to twenty-four.

There are many differences between where I live now and Chicago, where I grew up, not least of which is my status here as a member of an extreme minority. There are fundamental aspects to country life that I never considered when I lived in an urban setting. I buy food at the single small grocery store near the highway. The electric power grid crashes when it storms. Four-wheel drive is required to get from my house to the road when it snows—and it snows a lot. I'm wary of the bear that regularly rifles through my garbage can. And I must go to the post office in person to collect my mail, which is where I had an experience that is indelibly etched in my mind.

I usually go to the post office once a week, on Friday. On this particular day, I collected my mail as usual, returned without incident to my car, and prepared to head home. As I paused to wait for traffic before exiting the parking lot, a man pulled up beside me in a silver SUV. After some moments, I realized he was staring at me.

My "white people alert system" revved up. I jumped to the conclusion that this man was looking at me because I'm black. I hadn't been here long enough for it to be anything else. Although I'm fair-skinned, there is no way most people would mistake me for anything other than black.

Not wishing to give in to my paranoia, I smiled, as any neighbor would do. To my shock, he yelled the Obama invective at me and sped off, tires spitting gravel.

I was speechless. Why did this man target me? Was it the Obama sticker on my bumper? Was it my Illinois license plate (Obama's home state)? Does he think black people were solely responsible for electing Barack Obama to be the first African American president of the United States? Do I represent all black people in his mind? Would he have said the same thing to a white person?

No, I don't think so.

I don't think so because I have been trained to look at almost everything through the prism of race. My reactions to many incidents in life have been honed by years of communal black experience. We are taught to be wary; suspicious that every comment has hidden racial connotations and that every act is racially motivated. I don't yell "race" at every turn. I do not think of myself as a victim. I don't blame others for human failings that I am rightfully responsible for. However, I have a whole deck of race cards I can play at a moment's notice. I have an ever-present, oppressive feeling that never allows me to be totally comfortable.

Within my lifetime, not thinking about race could get you raped, beaten, killed. Stop after dark to use a toilet or eat in a "sundown" town and you could end up arrested or disappear forever. Walk in the wrong neighborhood in Chicago and you could be attacked by white people wielding baseball bats. The FBI compiled a report in 2009 of 3,816 cases of race-inspired hate crimes for that year alone; 83 percent of the victims were people of color.

White people are people to fear because they have no compunction about hurting you—with words or physical violence. This lesson has been reinforced over and over. Heeding it enabled us to survive. It is hard to purge.

In my younger years, I would have followed his white ass and given him a piece of my mind. Today, I merely record his face and car in my memory. In a country with a generous mixture of neo-Nazis, Christian fundamentalists, white supremacists, and survivalists, I would be a fool to do anything else.

Don't get me wrong—there are many sensible white people throughout this country and in my town, like the checkers at the grocery store, the man who fixes my car, the real estate agent who rented my house to me, and my friendly neighbors next door. Yet inbred paranoia and constant wariness are the burdens I brought with me when Tom and I decided to take this journey. All I know is that I want to heal. I want to live in a community, a country, and a world where race is not the defining factor of who I am; my humanity is.

Tom's Story

When Sharon told me the story of the man at the post office, I too was shocked—and sad. As I thought about her experience, I considered several possibilities that might have contributed to this man's vitriolic outburst. In addition to maybe politics, probably sexism, definitely an upbringing in which he didn't learn common decency or respect, one obvious factor is racism. What bothered him more: having a black president or having a black woman living in his almost-completely-white town?

White people have a long history of ignorance and kneejerk reactions to anything that frightens us. I've certainly been there. But I know from my study of trauma and its long-term impacts that it is people who have been harmed that inflict harm on others. This harm is passed down through generations. Though I have empathy for racist people and the unhealed wounds they carry, they still must be held to account.

I am a white man who lives in a town that is very white, much like Sharon's. Because of my growing relationships with people of color, I'm more aware than ever before of the pervasiveness of the ongoing problem of race.

There is a long history of white people saying and doing stupid, racist, and horribly damaging things to people of color. When the transatlantic slave trade was abolished by the US government on January 1, 1808, many white people—including my distant relatives—ignored that law for a long time. The Ku Klux Klan, White Citizens Councils, and others waged a war of terror on black people well into the twentieth century.

Today, increasing membership in white supremacist organizations is a growing cause for alarm.

Irrational fear is a product of ignorance, leading people to say and do some pretty stupid things. We hear it regularly, even from high-profile people who should know better. During the 2008 presidential contest, Senator Harry Reid observed that candidate Obama could succeed in his campaign for president in part because he was "light skinned" and had "no Negro dialect." When former president Bill Clinton sought Senator Edward Kennedy's endorsement for Hillary Clinton's presidential bid, he told Kennedy that in the recent past, Obama would have been serving them coffee. Former Illinois governor Rod Blagojevich claimed to be blacker than Barack Obama. When Virginia governor Bob McDonnell apologized for leaving out any reference to slavery in his Confederate History Month proclamation in April 2010, Mississippi governor Haley Barbour dismissed the controversy, sneering that it "doesn't amount to diddly." Kentucky senator Rand Paul compared himself to "idealists" like the Reverend Martin Luther King Jr., while at the same time expressing his conviction that private businesses should be allowed to turn away customers because of their race.

Thank goodness I'm not like any of *those* white people, but one of the good ones. After all, I wrote a book about my family's commitment to truth, justice, and undoing racism. *Inheriting the Trade* documents my descent from the largest slave-trading dynasty in US history and the journey I took with nine distant cousins to retrace the triangular route of the slave trade from Rhode Island to Ghana and Cuba. I speak at colleges and conferences around the country about the legacy of slavery and its present-day consequences, share progressive articles with friends on Facebook, and regularly write blog posts about these issues. Sitting at my desk in Oregon—which has a population that is 90 percent white, and in 1857 voted to ratify the state constitution with a provision that prohibited black people from moving here—I write about stupid white people who live somewhere else.

But the hard truth is that I *am* like other white people. As Pema Chödrön so powerfully wrote in her book, *The Places That Scare You*, "Compassion is not a relationship between the healer and the wounded. It's a relationship between equals. Only when we know our own darkness well can we be present with the darkness of others. Compassion becomes real when we recognize our shared humanity."

We all inherit damage from the past. We spread it like a virus and don't generally think about it. Too often, we just act. In December 2007, I participated in a three-day workshop led by Crossroads Anti-Racism Organizing and Training. The most powerful moment in an enlightening weekend came on the last day. Harold Fields, a man I count among my close friends, expressed how the white folks, with all our good intentions, continued to isolate and marginalize him and the other people of color in the room. What?! How could he include me in this company?

But Harold was right. The privilege I possess as a white man makes it easy for me to remain blissfully unaware of the negative impact I might have on others.

I realize, of course, that white people aren't the only ones who do and say stupid things. Black and brown folks do, too. It's simply that I know more about white folks because I *am* white folks. We've perpetrated a great deal of damage. And because of that legacy I believe we have a responsibility to acknowledge, speak out, and work to repair it.

When we begin holding each other accountable, committing our time to undoing injustice and inequality, and respecting each other in all our rich diversity, we will begin the process of healing the brokenness of our society. When we spend as much time learning about ourselves, our history, and all we have in common as we do watching "reality" television and trying to convince ourselves we're nothing like those *other* people, the world will become a richer, more harmonious place.

We embarked on this journey because we believe America must overcome the racial barriers that divide us; the barriers that drive us to strike out at one another out of ignorance and fear. To do nothing is unacceptable to us. The legacy of slavery remains a horrendous and unhealed wound, a disease that must be diagnosed, treated, and cured. We believe the approach we share in these pages may just make it possible to heal.

This is the story of two people who decided to try.

PART ONE

Crossing the Rubicon

"The world cannot be healed in the abstract. . . .
Healing begins where the wound was made."

ALICE WALKER
The Way Forward Is with a Broken Heart

CHAPTER ONE

The Recalcitrant Bat

Tom bolts straight upright in bed, startled from sleep by the screeching of a bird. The shriek is unlike any he's ever heard. He glances at the luminous clock in the pitch-dark room. The red numbers glow 3:39. All the windows are open, which makes it easy to hear the chirps, crows, and tweets of a wide variety of other, less-noisy feathered creatures. The natural symphony is further punctuated by the loud rattle of ancient, single-paned windows bombarded by forceful tropical winds. Tom glances at his wife Lindi, who continues to sleep peacefully next to him. This is the only time, he thinks, when her hearing disability is a blessing. The curtain across the room from the foot of their bed flaps violently outside its open portal. Tom slips through the opening in the mosquito netting that cocoons Lindi and him. He pulls the curtain back inside and closes the window. He takes a deep breath and climbs back under the covers.

Tom's heart rate slows back to normal as he finds his bearings on this first night in a strange room in a foreign country, Tobago, more than four thousand miles from home. The hypnotic sounds and steady roaring of the wind soon lull him back to sleep; as deep and restful as before.

Then, a few moments after 7:30, the storm outside reaches new heights of fury. Rain pours relentlessly from the sky. The sash that previously held one curtain in place in the sitting room next to the bedroom is gone; blown to some unknown destination outside. But it isn't the storm that awakens Tom this time. It is another crashing sound, coming from within the house.

Wham! Wham! Wham!

With sleep still in her eyes, Sharon emerges from the bedroom across the entry hall from Tom and Lindi's to find their host, Professor Hollis R. Lynch, in his pajamas, wielding a broom. He is beating it against the rafters. Tom joins Sharon in the great hall to witness the spectacle of a man on a mission. Lindi mercifully continues her slumber.

"Sorry for the racket," Professor Lynch announces between swings, "I must dislodge this recalcitrant bat!"

Wham! Wham!

"You see him way up there?"

They look up to see the small brown creature, snug in the uppermost corner of the ceiling's peak.

"Usually, I can dislodge them with a few whacks from the broom, but this little fellow is a stubborn one." Wham! The professor is determined to roust the bat and send it on its way. "If it becomes comfortable, not only will it likely return again but it might well start nesting . . . " Wham! " . . . with companions!"

"Being nocturnal," he further explains, "they hunt for food outside during the night. With the rising of the sun, they seek dark, little corners in which to sleep."

With six bedrooms, attached sitting rooms, a massive kitchen, lounge, and dining hall—most with high, pitched ceilings of dark wood—there are many such corners in this great house. When Hollis Lynch entered for the first time as its owner, bats were ensconced, thousands deep, in the dark recesses of this room. Their caustic guano has marred the rich mahogany floor. He has been fending them off ever since.

The contest ends in victory, the bat vanquished by Professor Lynch's invincible will. Though he tries to scare the small creature toward a window, the bat refuses to leave of its own accord. The professor ultimately smacks it with the broom and catches the stunned creature in a dustpan. Tossed outside from a balcony to the walkway some ten feet below, the bat trembles a few times, draws one last breath, and expires before our eyes.

As we gaze upon the dying creature, it dawns on both of us that this little bat appeared at a fortuitous moment. It becomes a metaphor for racism and why we have come so far, to this particular island in the Caribbean.

The seeds for this journey were planted long before we arrived. Sharon says they were sown by ancestral spirits who call us to our healing work.

Will Hairston is a white man who descends from one of the largest slave-holding empires in the Old South. The story of his family's complex web of relationships over many generations, from being slave owners through the recent past, is told in Henry Wiencek's book *The Hairstons: An American Family in Black and White.*

When he was eighteen years old, Will attended the annual family reunion of the "Hairston Clan," an eight-hundred-person-strong gathering of an African American family with roots in the South and a direct connection to Will. The Hairstons have been convening family reunions since 1931. In 1980, they invited Waller Staples Hairston, Will's father, to join them as their guest speaker at the Hyatt Regency Hotel in Washington, DC. Will accompanied his father.

Waller Hairston descended from a dynasty that, at its height, controlled nine plantations—encompassing upwards of forty farms—stretching from the tidewaters of Virginia to the backwoods of Mississippi. Many thousands of African American people worked their lands as slaves, making them one of the richest families in the antebellum South. It was only recently that black and white Hairstons would have gathered for such an affair. It is a story that few from the family's storied past would have ever believed possible.

Seventy-nine-year-old Jester Hairston, the noted composer, songwriter, and actor, was there. He led the singing of his song, *Amen,* made famous in the 1963 film *Lilies of the Field.*

Will was transformed. The experience of the reunion, of being with the descendants of people his ancestors had once enslaved, of being welcomed and accepted there, changed his life. He witnessed the power of song, of coming together, and of connection with a family much larger than he had ever known.

And then there is Susan Hutchison. Susan is the six-times-great-granddaughter of President Thomas Jefferson and his wife, Martha. In

2003, after exploring her family history—and its deep connection to slavery—she attended an unlikely family reunion as well. Hers was with the descendants of Jefferson and Sally Hemings, the woman he enslaved on his Monticello plantation and who bore several of his children. At the reunion, Susan met Henry Wiencek. Having experienced the power of reunion, she told him she wanted to meet other white descendants of families who had enslaved people.

Henry introduced Susan to Will. Together, they came up with the idea of a family reunion that was vastly different from what most people are accustomed to. It would not be a meeting of just one family. It would be a reunion that involved multiple families from both sides of the racial construct; a reunion of black and white—the descendants of people who were slaveholders with the descendants of those whom they had enslaved.

Their idea was based on one key acknowledgment: Be they black, white or mixed, families are families. America's legacy of slavery ripped apart untold numbers of family bonds. Not only were African American families broken; white families were estranged as well. From the time slavery was instituted in the United States, black and white generations had lived and died together. They often had children together. But there was profound alienation on both sides of the racial divide. Far too many white Americans were in denial, believing that the wounds of the past had been healed by the civil rights movement of the 1960s.

To begin understanding the impact of slavery, one must consider F. George Kay's words in his book *The Shameful Trade*: "The purchase or capture of some fifty million human beings month in and month out [over] a period of four centuries was perhaps the greatest crime against humanity ever perpetrated by Christendom, not least because those responsible for the most part saw no moral evil in treating men, women, and children as merchandise."

Susan and Will saw building relationships with the "other side" as a path toward a future where the deep wounds engendered by slavery could be confronted and potentially reconciled. They were inspired by Dr. Martin Luther King Jr.'s words, spoken from the steps of the Lincoln Memorial on August 28, 1963: "I have a dream that one day on the red hills of Georgia the sons of former slaves and the sons of former slave owners will be able to sit down together at the table of brotherhood."

Fired with resolve, Will and Susan invited their cousins to share another observation made by Dr. King: "We are caught in an inescapable network of mutuality, tied in a single garment of destiny." Under their leadership, black and white Jeffersons and Hairstons began planning a revolution. A group now known as Coming to the Table was born.

An experience was planned in which black and white descendants of ancestors linked by a slave/slave-owner relationship, a blood connection, or both could explore the history of slavery—its legacy and impact on their lives. They had a longer-term goal to create a model of healing to guide individuals and groups that continue to struggle with racism in the United States and throughout the world.

Forty-two years after Dr. King shared his dream, two dozen descendants from both sides of the system of enslavement gathered at the table. That first small retreat took place in January 2006 at Eastern Mennonite University (EMU) in Harrisonburg, Virginia, where Will works. Through sharing stories and building relationships, the participants embraced King's dream: They began to envision a more connected and truthful society that would be eager to address the unresolved and persistent effects of the institution of slavery.

From the beginning, EMU supported the work of Coming to the Table. It fit well with the university's peacebuilding mission. It adopted the program, designated a manager, and sought funding. Two and a half years later, the university's Center for Justice and Peacebuilding offered an official weeklong Coming to the Table course of study as part of the Summer Peacebuilding Institute. We both attended. It opened the doorway to our collaboration and profoundly affected both our lives.

Tom's Story

In the middle of a cold, snowy winter in January 2011, my wife and I fly to New York. Sharon, Lindi, and I will travel together from there to Tobago. I've been listening to Daniel Defoe's *Robinson Crusoe* on my iPod. Sharon had mentioned that Tobago was the island Defoe envisioned when he wrote his novel three hundred years ago. I had seen a movie version decades ago but never read the book. *Robinson Crusoe* is one of those tales that Mark Twain described as a classic: one that people praise but haven't read.

I was surprised to learn that the character Crusoe was an English slave-trader, even though he himself had been enslaved for a time in North Africa. He later owned a plantation and enslaved people in Brazil. After a few prosperous years there, Crusoe's knowledge of Africa and the slave trade led a group of businessmen to ask him to accompany them on a voyage to the Guinea coast to buy more Africans. Crusoe agreed. Shortly after they left Brazil, they encountered a ferocious storm that sank their ship. All but one perished: Robinson Crusoe, the sole survivor, made it ashore where he spent most of the next twenty-eight years alone. He was joined for the final few years by the person who became his servant; the man he called Friday.

Many of the filmed versions of Defoe's novel make no mention of Crusoe's involvement with slavery and the slave trade. As scholars have done with many history books, screenwriters and directors chose to hide the more unsavory aspects of Defoe's story.

A CARIBBEAN IDYLL

The first breath one takes upon disembarking from the plane is the memorable one. The warm, tropical air provides enchanting relief after the recycled oxygen of a five-hour flight. It instantly banishes the chill of the Oregon and New York we left behind. It is magical and healing. We spread our arms to expand our lung capacity and breathe in deeply.

The Republic of Trinidad and Tobago comprises the two southern-most islands in the Caribbean archipelago, 1,520 miles south of Bermuda, the northernmost. The first permanent settlers, who established themselves thousands of years before Europeans arrived, were Amerindians from the South American continent. Much of Tobago still looks as it did in 1498, when Columbus named it Bellaforma without ever setting foot on its beaches.

The two islands of this shared nation could not be more different. They developed separately and have little in common other than their natural beauty. In Tobago, no fewer than thirty-one colonial changes of power took place as different European countries vied to control its re-sources. It ping-ponged between the French and the British in 1763 and again in 1803, after which it remained under British control until Trini-dad and Tobago obtained independence as one nation in 1962.

Tobago is the smaller of the two islands. Cigar shaped, it is roughly twenty-six miles long by seven miles wide—with the warm, calm Caribbean Sea on one side and the cooler, rough Atlantic Ocean on the other. The name derives from the word *tovaco* (tobacco) in the language of the original Amerindian inhabitants. The spine of the island, a 14,000-acre rainforest, is the world's oldest legally protected preserve, set aside in 1776 to gather rain for the sugar plantations.

Trinidad is populated largely by two groups—people of African descent (39 percent) and East Indian descent (40 percent). Tobago's population, on the other hand, is 99 percent African descent. There are more than 1.2 million residents on Trinidad and 54,000 on Tobago.[1] Trinidad is industrial, with a focus on oil and natural gas reserves. Tobago remains largely agricultural but has recently begun to promote tourism.

The primary reason we are coming to Tobago is to have extended, focused writing time together, away from the business of our everyday lives. A sojourn here will enable us to revisit a significant "scene of the crime" in the transatlantic slave trade. Another draw was the ambience of life on a Caribbean island.

Sharon's son is married to the daughter of our host, the owner of Richmond Great House, which will be our home for the next two weeks. We can write unimpeded, with the added benefit of an African history scholar in residence.

The man who built Richmond House was Walter Pringle, who received a land grant from the British Crown around 1760. His mission was to carve out a successful sugar plantation at a time when the value of sugar rivaled that of gold. His efforts were supported by every resource within the purview of the British Empire.

As elsewhere in the Caribbean and the Americas, African slave labor was the key to financial success in Tobago. As Susan Craig-James records in *A Fractured Whole: The Changing Society of Tobago, 1838–1938*: "The production of sugar, largely on the basis of slave labor, to which most of the Caribbean region was devoted from the mid-seventeenth century until well into the nineteenth century was integral to European expansion and the development of the modern world economy." In 1791, the total population of the island was 15,102. Ninety-four percent of the inhabitants were enslaved.

Our drive from the airport takes about half an hour along twisting, narrow Windward Road. As we approach our destination, the driver turns left at a sign that reads "Richmond Great House." Across the road, another metal sign swings in the breeze. It advertises Carib, the local beer. The quarter-mile driveway winds up a steep incline to the house. We park in front of the grand entryway, a curved dual-sided stone staircase.

Professor Lynch emerges from the double doors at the top of the stairs and descends down the right side to greet us.

"Welcome! Welcome!" he announces, in his proper English accent.

We lug our bags upstairs. Room assignments are established. Food is unpacked into cupboards, the refrigerator, and freezer. Unscreened windows are open throughout the house. The crosscurrent of breezes is cool and refreshing.

Richmond Great House is situated atop a hill with a panoramic view of the Atlantic Ocean. Built sometime around 1766, it is a marvel, from the peaked roof to the hardwood floors. The roof overhang prevents the most aggressive rain or direct sunlight from intruding into the house. The all-around windows often remain open to the elements day and night, negating the need for air-conditioning.

One of the few surviving plantation houses on Tobago, it is the oldest by at least a century. The plantation once manufactured sugar, molasses, and rum until the industry collapsed in the late nineteenth century. The owners at that time diversified into cocoa and coconuts. Cadbury Schweppes, the British confectioner, was at one time a joint venture partner.

The original estate that encompassed Richmond House—some five hundred acres—was one of more than eighty similar landholdings. Together they comprised an intricate plantation system that continued to thrive into the mid-twentieth century, long after slavery ended.

Henry Iles Woodcock's 1866 *History of Tobago* tells us that, when the land commissioner sold the first plots, it was stipulated that "for every one hundred acres of land cleared the purchaser should keep one white man or two white women" in residence. The average sale price per acre was slightly more than two pounds sterling. The death knell of the plantation system wasn't heard until 1963, when Hurricane Flora wiped out most of the great houses, along with their crops.

Hollis Lynch bought Richmond Great House in 1973. The previous owners had decided to sell after an unsuccessful attempt to restore the estate after Flora's rampage. Dr. Lynch, a native of Tobago and, at that time, a professor of African History at Columbia University in New York City, heard about the sale and, almost on a lark, decided to buy it. He arranged financing through a bank in Tobago with which he had done business for many years.

"But the owner would never sell to me," says the professor. "He did all he could to block the sale. My bank called and the forthcoming financing was canceled." Fortunately, the obdurate owner had lost control of the property. A different white man, the representative from Cadbury, was in charge. He consummated the sale of the colonial house with six acres of land to Professor Lynch. "The Cadbury man had no connection to the old colonial system and its network of people here. He didn't care that I was black, only that I had the financial wherewithal to complete the purchase."

Over the next three decades, the professor refurbished and improved the house and the property, carefully preserving its character and historical features. Richmond Great House is now an established historic landmark. It is filled with antique furnishings and African artifacts the professor has acquired in his international travels.

The resistant European owner and his wife continued to live elsewhere on Tobago for the rest of the man's life. "I've met his children," says Professor Lynch. "His grandson came here one day to show his girlfriend around. Surprise! She was a black girl! Young people today, you see, have very little problem with race."

In light of our reason for being here, his comment feels ironic. We marvel at the poignancy of being in a former slave plantation—a black woman and a white man trying to make sense of the journey we have undertaken.

Our laptops rest on one of four tables in the main hall. Piles of books, from among the thousands in the professor's library, surround us. We have the luxury of an incredible assortment of rare volumes. It is a perfect place for research and reflection.

Our large rooms are located at the front of the house, with separate sitting rooms in each. Antique four-poster beds dominate the bedrooms. They are so tall we need step stools to climb into them. Before tucking in for the night, we hang the mosquito nets we brought with us from New York. The arduous journey has left us tired but expectant about what lies ahead. We fall asleep easily, lulled by intoxicating night winds. The moon is almost full; shining bright in the clear, dark sky, surrounded by more stars than these three foreigners ever see in brightly lit American cities.

The next morning, after the ordeal with the bat, we both lean back in our chairs and stare at the pitched ceiling above our heads where the creature attempted to perch. It occurs to us that racism and the legacy of slavery share certain characteristics with the little bat. They are both ubiquitous and persistent. They hide from the light of day. They thrive in packs of like-minded creatures. They drop guano everywhere. Racism is a remarkably tenacious and resilient plague that seldom departs on its own. Those who seek to heal must pursue their goal as relentlessly as the professor pursued his prey.

CHAPTER TWO

Castaways from Security Island

Tom's Story

My earliest memories include bigger-than-life fantasies of the profound future impact I would surely have on the world. Watching John Wayne's heroics on the silver screen led me to imagine my Oscar acceptance speech by age thirteen. My father and Dick Wing, the youth minister at our church, talked me out of pursuing acting as a profession. My next mission was to follow in Billy Graham's footsteps and become a preacher. I attended Dick's alma mater, Northwest Christian College in Eugene, Oregon, with that goal in mind. After I'd been there for a few years, it became clear that the ministry was also not my calling.

I returned to my first love: the movies, opening Pat & Mike's Cinema & Restaurant in downtown Bend, Oregon, with two partners. Our customers watched provocative, offbeat movies as they ate burgers and sipped cold beers. I acted in plays with a local community theater group and opened a video rental store that our family operated for thirteen years.

Though I long ago recognized that another childhood fantasy—becoming president of the United States—was as likely as my becoming the next John Wayne or Billy Graham, I did enter local politics to make a positive difference in my community. After more than a decade in public office, I resigned and focused my full-time attention to completing my first book.

Well into my fifties, I joked that I was still trying to figure out what I wanted to be when I grew up. Never would I have imagined that I would "find" myself through a combination of visits to two places that were so completely dissimilar. The first awakening was in a slave dungeon in Cape Coast Castle, on the rocky shoreline of Ghana, whose exit was the notorious "Door of No Return" for millions of enslaved Africans. It was there that I learned the meaning of utter despair. The other was at Eastern Mennonite University in Virginia's Shenandoah Valley, where I encountered hope.

As I think about that first long weekend in January 2006, when two dozen people gathered at EMU, I can't imagine what my life would be today without that experience. We learned a bit about neuroscience and the brain, and explored the concept of healing from trauma and the importance of storytelling in building and nurturing relationships. Even more than the presentations from experts, the heart of the experience was in the stories we shared.

For dinner one evening, my cousins Dain and Constance Perry and I joined Joe Henry Hairston and other members of the Hairston family; Ever Lee Hairston and Lillie and Jim Brown.

Constance was really jazzed: "This whole weekend is the next best thing to talking about these important issues with my own family."

"You and I have an advantage that many black people don't," said Joe. "You and I didn't grow up feeling subhuman." He and Constance had both grown up in the North.

"It's drilled into you every day," said Ever Lee, who grew up in South Carolina. " 'You won't amount to anything.' 'You can't do things.' "

Constance told about being at a conference in Greenville, Mississippi. She and a colleague, a white woman, asked for a recommendation for a restaurant. "Everyone said, 'Go to Doe's. People come from all over the state to go there.' So we went and I was the only black person there. I will never forget the stare from one man. His glare said, 'You don't belong here.' It was devastating. He took my sense of 'me' away. I can't imagine facing that every day."

"But of course," said Ever Lee.

Lillie, Jim, and Joe nodded in understanding.

With gray hair and a confident smile, Joe looked younger than his eighty-three years. He had fought in World War II and Korea. "I was one of the first blacks at my base in the South. I overheard two crackers on the corner: 'Looks like some Northern niggers. We need to teach them how to act.' That was my first experience in the South. I'd never experienced racism like this before.

"I live in Washington, DC now and I grew up in Pittsburgh. I was an orphan very young. I had a horrible home life, but I lived in a great neighborhood. I was raised by several families. We all came from different backgrounds. I remember a Polish woman who would spank me like I was one of her own if I stepped out of line. We kids were all treated the same. I never felt inferior."

Although many warm friendships were born that weekend, it would be two and a half years before I would be together with any of these people again. When I returned to EMU for the Summer Peacebuilding Institute session in June 2008, I would meet someone else who reminds me of Joe Henry and Constance. Like them, Sharon Morgan was raised in the North and has stories to share. Little did I know that one day soon, she and I would embark on a journey that would change our lives.

Sharon's Story

Although I'm not big on joining organizations, I've always been outspoken about my beliefs and willing to mobilize people to do things. In my profession, I generally try to marry corporate interests with community good.

In 1985, I was part of a team that promoted the first celebration of the Reverend Martin Luther King Jr.'s birthday as a national holiday. As vice president of the advertising agency at which McDonald's was a client, we developed a program for the fast-food chain to commemorate the holiday. It included a television entertainment special, museum exhibits, and a curriculum kit. When the program ended, the collection of personal artifacts was put on permanent display at Hartsfield-Jackson Atlanta International Airport. The exhibit is still there and I am proud to have played a major part in making the program a reality as project manager.

One of my responsibilities was traveling with Mrs. Coretta Scott King. It was she who told me that her husband much preferred the "Rev."

designation in front of his name rather than "Dr." He was far more proud of serving God than man.

By the time I reached Coming to the Table, I'm not sure whether I found it or it found me. There has always been a disquieting feeling inside me that has much to do with race. Racial acrimony, devolving to us all as a result of America's foundation in slavery, is a fatal flaw in the American consciousness. For more than three decades, I have been exploring my roots in that morass. My disquiet has grown ever more insistent with the passing years.

As a young child, I never received a satisfactory answer about what "color" I was. When I asked my grandmother, she "hmphed." My mother declined to answer. In elementary school, my favorite nun added to my confusion when, in speaking about genetics, she described one of my friends as a "freak" because she had brown skin, green eyes, and long, straight hair. What was I to surmise from that—me with almost white skin, brown eyes, and kinky hair? My mother was "white" to the eyes; my father, dark brown. My close relatives run the gamut from white skin and flaming red hair to chocolate brown with black eyes.

I remember when black people first started appearing on television. It is hard to imagine now, but most people didn't have televisions until well into the 1950s. We had one. Whenever somebody black was scheduled to appear, the whole neighborhood was on alert. In 1956, Nat King Cole was the first black performer to host a variety series on network television. NBC canceled the show after thirteen months for lack of a national sponsor. Companies were afraid of the racial dynamics of the program and how it would play in the South.

Most of the programs we watched featured perfect white families like *Ozzie and Harriett* and *Father Knows Best*. Black people were represented by the buffoonery of *Amos and Andy* and Jack Benny's eye-rolling sidekick, Rochester. We laughed at these programs because they were all we had. But imagine the effect of such pervasively negative images for black children. White children were affirmed every day with the *Mickey Mouse Club* and *Romper Room*.

My interest in genealogy began in 1969, the year my son was born. I wanted to find out where I came from and provide that legacy to my son. The only thing I could pass on was the resilience I knew had come from our history as slaves. Physical slavery inhibited us from the start. By the time I came along, in spite of cries that "Black is beautiful," the slavery was psychological.

Since then, I have traveled thousands of miles in search of my ancestors. I have walked centuries-old cemeteries, devoured obscure genealogical books in libraries, and studied crumbling records in archives and courthouses in Alabama, Mississippi, and other Southern states. In 2007, I created a website—Our Black Ancestry—to help others follow their family journeys through history. A reference to Coming to the Table popped up one day among the information I regularly cull for news items to post on my website.

What caught my attention was a story about linked descendants, progeny of people who had been enslaved and the people who enslaved them had come together, reaching across a chasm of indifference to connect with a painful part of their families' past. It wasn't some rhetorical past, it was a personal past, one in which their ancestors—black and white—had been active participants.

I leaned closer to my computer screen. This was unbelievable! Having come from a family where people on both sides had borne the dehumanization of enslavement, I had often wondered how—or if—I would have endured the experience. Would I have worked in the big house or out in the field? Would I have been docile and defeated or belligerent and rebellious? Would I have been whipped? Raped? Forced to bear children who would also have been enslaved? Would I have died young from overwork and been tossed into an unmarked grave? Would I have run away? Killed myself? Killed my master and his family by slipping tiny shards of glass in their soup?

We all like to think we would not have succumbed to such a diminished state. But when we ponder the past, we transport the person we are today into a scenario that bears scant resemblance to contemporary society. I can't know what I would have experienced or how I would have reacted. The one thing I do know—and feel to my core—is that whatever happened was violent and ugly, the wrongest of wrongs. Here was a story about people who had decided to confront it—together.

I fired off an e-mail to Amy Potter, the name in the "contact us" box on the website. I received a warm response. Amy and I wrote to each other for almost a year. Eventually, she invited me to participate in a five-day class being offered in June 2008 through the Summer Peacebuilding Institute at Eastern Mennonite University. She explained that the focus of the course was to educate participants in recognizing and healing from the trauma of the legacy of slavery. To say that I was intrigued would be an understatement.

EMU is nestled among the hills in the Shenandoah Valley of western Virginia, in the small city of Harrisonburg. It is far removed from the Alabama and Mississippi I know; and farther still—both geographically and psychologically—from my hometown of Chicago. Virginia is the veritable heart of the country; the place where both America and slavery were born, as well as the capital of the Confederate secession.

I was skeptical about going to a Mennonite institution. I knew nothing about Mennonites, except my assumption that they were universally white and outside the pale of mainstream religious denominations. Thinking of the Amish, I halfway expected to encounter men in big black hats driving buggies and women wearing bonnets and nineteenth-century dresses.

Although the concept certainly sounded interesting, I was ambivalent about participating. Is it really possible to heal from a terrible trauma that is centuries old? What if I encountered a bunch of whiny, wingnut, white apologists? Did I really want to spend a week with white people I didn't know in a place that reeked of historic malfeasance? No, I did not.

My curiosity had been piqued, but I decided not to spend my hard-earned money or devote my precious time engaging such a ponderous bundle of unknowns. The thought of driving seven hundred miles resurrected age-old parental admonishments about traveling by car only in daylight, carrying toilet paper so we could pee in the bushes, eating only at restaurants that prominently advertised "soul food," and driving straight through with no stopovers, especially in any town that included "white" in its name.

I'm not naturally an angry or violent person. I believe profoundly in God and the magnificence of His creations, but I have personal knowledge of how some others don't always feel the same. I've been warned, well into the twenty-first century, to be very—*very*—careful, wandering the backroads of the South. I keep a shotgun in my car and, once I cross the Mason-Dixon Line, I prefer to travel with trusted friends. Even then, I rarely travel at night.

Amy encouraged me to reconsider with the inducement of a scholarship and free lodging. She assured me I would be welcomed and that my contributions would be listened to and respected. My reluctance melted.

PEACE AND JUSTICE

Neither of us had heard of Eastern Mennonite University prior to our encounter with Coming to the Table. We'd heard of Mennonites, of course, but as Sharon wrote, we knew very little about this branch of Christianity or why a group dedicated to healing the wounds of racism born of slavery would be founded and headquartered at a Mennonite institution. Now that we know more, it's easy to understand the connection.

The Mennonite Church was founded in the sixteenth century. After the printing press was invented around 1455, the Bible was one of the first books to be mass-produced. As people attained literacy, they read the Bible and began to interpret it for themselves. Thus began trouble for the men in positions of power within the Catholic Church. For the first time, the sheep in the flock could actually think for themselves. This led to the Protestant Reformation. Martin Luther and John Calvin broke from the Catholic Church. Each formed a new "Protestant" church.

A short time later, Menno Simons, an ordained Catholic priest, rejected Catholicism and joined the Anabaptists, who did not consider themselves Protestants, but a separate, radical reformation of the Catholic faith. Anabaptists believed in the baptism of adults rather than infants; that people should join the church and be baptized only when they were mature enough to make the conscious decision that they believed in Jesus and desired to live as he commanded. They believed in complete separation of religion and government. They had an absolute belief in nonviolence and peace. Thousands of early Anabaptists were martyred for refusing to renounce their beliefs, offering no resistance.

Several existing denominations trace their roots to the Anabaptists, including the Amish, Brethren in Christ, and Mennonites. Mennonites number approximately 1 million adherents worldwide, with 150,000 in the United States. Sharon's assumption regarding the racial makeup of

Mennonite churches in the United States is correct. Close to 90 percent of its members are white.[1]

It is the Mennonite commitment to peace that resonates with our work and that of Coming to the Table. This commitment is embodied at EMU in the Center for Justice and Peacebuilding, which offers a graduate program in conflict transformation, the Summer Peacebuilding Institute, and the STAR (Strategies for Trauma Awareness & Resilience) program. Many one-week courses are offered for people who have "regular" lives but want to increase their peacebuilding skills.

Tom's Story

During the two and a half years since my first visit to EMU, I stayed connected with many of my newfound Coming to the Table friends via e-mail. We shared information and grew relationships. I finished writing *Inheriting the Trade*; it was published by Beacon Press. *Traces of the Trade*, the film of our family journey, premiered at the Sundance Film Festival in January 2008.

In June of that same year, I flew back to Harrisonburg. I'd heard that EMU has international appeal, but had no idea of the extent. There were 105 students from forty-six different countries in attendance that week. Clearly, oppression knows no national boundaries. They came to study conflict resolution, restorative justice, social change, reconciliation, healing from trauma, and other peacebuilding subjects.

I met a woman from Uganda who was taking a different class. Her children had been kidnapped by the Lord's Resistance Army, a bizarre, fundamentalist Christian guerrilla group that seeks to establish a theocracy based on the Ten Commandments. They are one of the most brutal and inhumane movements to ever exist in Africa. One of her kidnapped daughters was missing for years. Before being released, she was repeatedly raped by her captors and gave birth to three children. Her mother forgave those who perpetrated this horrific crime against her family. She's now helping to raise her grandchildren.

I wonder how something like this is even possible to survive, let alone forgive. I contemplate what centuries of the slave trade followed by European colonization have contributed to present-day horrors in Uganda and other African nations, not to mention the United States.

Sixteen of us—all from the United States—gathered for the weeklong course on the Coming to the Table model of healing. I met almost half the participants for the first time. I looked forward to studying restorative justice and digging more deeply into understanding trauma; specifically historic trauma and how it is passed down from generation to generation.

One of my classmates was a man I met here in 2006. On December 9, 2007—just six months prior to our class—David Works's family was leaving church in Colorado Springs when a young man opened fire and began randomly shooting people. Two of David's daughters were killed. David was shot twice but survived.

David shared with our group how he thought about the trauma response in "Cycles of Violence," to which we were introduced in 2006 (see illustration in "Notes on Methodology" at the end of this book). Two circles—one labeled "Victim" and the other "Aggressor"—form an infinity symbol. The common reaction to unaddressed traumatic experiences is to get trapped in one or both cycles. You enter the victim cycle when you turn your unhealed traumatic wounds against yourself through alcohol and drug abuse, overwork, depression, etc. You enter the aggressor cycle when you act out against others with physical or psychological abuse, revenge, intolerance, etc. Whether the trauma is "acted in" against the self or "acted out" against others, the effects are transmitted from one generation to the next. The Trauma Healing Journey taught at EMU focuses on breaking free of the cycles of violence.

David's family used these principles, along with their faith, to break out of potentially destructive cycles in order to have a chance to heal. David says that the grief they experienced was messy and unpredictable, and may never go away. Trauma is unique to each individual.

Over the course of our week together, and in community with people taking other classes, I was offered a variety of perspectives on the lingering damage we all inherit. The collective and individual trauma of the past includes the legacy of slavery. Added to that is the trauma we experience during our own lifetimes.

I met Sharon Morgan that week for the first time and, to be honest; we didn't hit it off right away—not sure why. After all, she's quite a bit like me: funny, loud, sarcastic, brash, and certainly self-confident. I just remember she sat on one side of the room, I on the other; and she seemed guarded, a bit standoffish, perhaps a little intimidating. Though there was no outright antagonism, we interacted little. For whatever reasons, our relationship didn't begin with an instant connection. We met. We learned together. We parted.

Then we hooked up on Facebook and discovered our mutual interest in genealogy. I checked out her Our Black Ancestry website and found her far more passionate, knowledgeable, and dedicated to genealogical research than I am.

Five months later, in early November, I was a featured speaker at the Redemption of Reason conference at the University of Chicago, in Sharon's hometown. Sharon drove to the auditorium just to greet me and give me a hug before rushing off to her evening plans. If I were to identify a moment at which our relationship began to blossom, that was it.

Sharon's Story

The first time I met Tom at EMU, I was taken aback by his intensity. He has these piercing blue eyes that he keeps trained on you, as if he is trying to see through you. As a child, I was taught it is impolite to stare. Black people in the generations before me learned to always avert their eyes when talking to white people. We tend to look away when we speak to you and then look at you when you speak to us. I have heard that white people think this is evidence of insincerity. In my experience, they are able to look anyone directly in the eye at any time—and be totally insincere with a straight face.

Tom takes a lot of notes, either on his computer or a notepad. During the week we spent in class together, I wasn't sure, even when he was staring at me, whether he was *really* paying attention to me or cataloging me.

The truth is that I didn't know where to place him and, in all honesty, didn't have a warm feeling. I was, however, intrigued. I had read his book before we met and was impressed with the broad concept as well as the way in which he treated his material. Here was a white man who really did "inherit the trade" and was bold enough to deal with it, not with arrogance but humility.

On top of that, he had journeyed to a place I longed to visit: Cape Coast Castle. Until I do, I can't completely fathom the experience. Sitting in the pitch-blackness of a men's dungeon, he had the opportunity, and sensitivity, to reflect on what few white men ever even think about. In *Inheriting the Trade*, he reflected, "For the first moment in my life I have an inkling of what total despair feels like. Unimaginable horror envelopes me, pierces me. Tears stream down my cheeks."

I think everyone should have that experience; black and white people alike. But especially white men.

I'm still not entirely sure what compelled me to go see Tom that night at the University of Chicago. I had other plans, but it was on my way. Something in my heart pushed me to do it, and I think maybe I just wanted to "touch" this intriguing person and see whether or not he was really serious about what he was doing. I admire people who write thoughtful books, and I very much admire someone who would expose himself as Tom did. He broached a topic that was dear to me and possibly dangerous to him. My experience is that white people don't generally want to talk about slavery—or anything else that exposes secrets with regard to race. I wanted to encourage his work but I wanted to do it gingerly.

DISCHARGING THE PAIN

One week after our quick hug in Chicago, we both attended a Reevaluation Counseling workshop in Seattle. As its website describes, RC is a process whereby people learn how to exchange help, or "co-counsel," with each other to help free them from the effects of past distress experiences. The theory assumes that people are born with great potential, are naturally loving, with a zest for life. These qualities become stifled as we grow up due to the accumulation of experiences involving fear, hurt, loss, pain, anger, embarrassment, and so on. By discharging the associated emotions during shared counseling sessions, participants can be freed from behavioral patterns and wounds caused by the hurt.

The purpose of this workshop, and two more that would be held in the months ahead, was to see how RC might fit within the Coming to the Table model of healing.

Sharon was appalled by the naked expressions of emotion. As she described it, "People were weepin' and wailin' all over the place—baring their souls to complete strangers." She absolutely did not feel comfortable expressing her emotions to people she didn't know—especially white people—and she didn't.

We both left Seattle with a great deal of skepticism, but our mutual discomfort turned out to be a catalyst for ongoing conversations. Then Sharon was selected to be a marketing and publicity resource for Coming to the Table and Tom was chosen to serve on the Advisory Board. Our connections to the organization—and to each other—grew.

Tom's Story

I agreed to attend the second RC training weekend in Richmond, Virginia, in April 2009. Sharon did not. This time I found many aspects of RC more valuable than I did in Seattle. It was presented in ways that made more sense. Then—surprise, surprise—a few months later, Sharon and I both committed to attend the third RC workshop in Jackson, Mississippi, in August. One thing stronger than our skepticism was our faith in Coming to the Table and its people. Sharon had a condition. Because of our past mutual skepticism, she asked that I be her co-counseling partner. I agreed. Our relationship evolved from "opposite sides of the room" to "up close and personal."

When I arrived at Jackson State, the historically black university where the workshop was held, I dropped my bags in my room and hustled over to the dining hall to grab dinner. Sharon sat with Rachel Noble, a member of the RC training team.

"How are you?" Rachel asked me.

"Well, to be blunt," I said, "my wife lost her job two days ago, and things are a bit challenging. As of yesterday, I wasn't sure I'd be here. But here I am."

Sharon just stared at me. "I lost my job on Friday. I almost canceled as well."

So here we were in the same boat: castaways from security island.

After Rachel left, I told Sharon I wanted to talk with her about something: "I've been thinking about writing a book about my experiences with Coming to the Table and decided it would be more effective if I could work with a coauthor. This project is all about people from both sides of the 'color line' coming together. Partnering with a woman would balance the gender aspect as well.

"You're a writer," I noted. "Based on the work you do, I figure you meet deadlines. You're committed to Coming to the Table and reconciliation. So . . ."

She laughed. "That is *not* what I expected you to say."

We agreed to mull it over.

The RC workshop turned out pretty well. There are aspects of it, such as creating safe spaces, building trust, and growing relationships, which we found valuable.

When we spoke by phone the week after the workshop about writing together, Sharon said yes. What evolved from subsequent conversations was the idea to build a purposeful relationship guided by the principles we had learned through Coming to the Table.

"We'll need to spend time together in each other's homes, with each other's families," Sharon observed.

"That's brilliant!" was my response. "You can come to lily-white Bend, Oregon, and I'll travel to Bronzeville in Chicago."

"If we're going to do this honestly, I will tell you things I've never said to white people before," she said. "I don't spend a lot of time around white people. They scare me."

Sharon struck me as courageous but apprehensive, willing but uncertain; again, a lot like me. I'm certain now that these were major factors that kept us from hitting it off initially. It felt like we'd agreed to jump from the high dive without checking for water in the pool. But we would dive together.

Sharon's Story

Sometimes, the best way to approach a huge problem is to take it in bite-sized pieces. For me, Tom DeWolf was one of those pieces. We embarked on an experiment to see how engaging in a meaningful platonic relationship with one person from "the other side" might embody a way forward for confronting issues of race.

We agreed to chart the evolution of our relationship within the context of racial reconciliation. A black woman and a white man would cross the threshold into each other's personal space, engage in the lives of both our families and friends. We intended to learn how and why our lives are different or similar and see if it would make any difference as we reached for the goal of healing.

Our upbringings could not have been more different. Tom is a middle-aged white man who grew up in California and has lived for many years in a snow-white community in the Pacific Northwest. I am a middle-aged black woman who grew up in Chicago in a neighborhood that most people would describe as a "ghetto." Today, I live in a rural, lily-white community on the East Coast that puts me in close proximity to my grandchildren in New York City. My new home has also given me opportunities to engage in social relationships with white people.

When we agreed to this project, my key concern was that this experience be mutually respectful while being truly engaging. I remember how, in the 1970s, it was popular for white people to "adopt" black people as "friends."

"It was a one-way street," I told Tom. "White people would invite you to parties and be nice to you at work. But it was very superficial. It was clear that black people were the ones who were expected to do all of the adjusting; all of the getting along. The relationships were largely forced and unnatural. At any moment it felt like you could expect to be told to leave the room."

A LEAP OF FAITH

We agreed to spend our first extended time with each other and our families in November 2009. It wasn't to be in either of our homes. Sharon flew to Los Angeles the Monday before Thanksgiving to spend the holiday with her cousin Renee Dixon and her family. They hadn't seen each other in more than two years. Tom would join them a few days later.

CHAPTER THREE

Friends on Purpose

Sharon's Story

I knew clearly why I had invited Tom to spend the week with my family
in California. Renee, her husband Eugene, and their children and grandchildren are different in significant ways from the rest of our family, who
remained in the Midwest. In general, they are more "free" in their way
of thinking and their lifestyles. Midwesterners are stoic and traditional.
Californians are more progressive. Spending time with the Dixons would
be exactly the right place to start our journey.

Tom wasn't with us on Thanksgiving Day—his loss. Eugene and I
did the shopping and, as we prepared dinner, we laughed over the fact
that Renee didn't inherit the family cooking genes. As the whole family
chopped, sautéed, and baked, we caught up on the last couple of years and
discussed my project with Tom. I told everybody my goal was for him to
witness what a great family we have and how we deal with race.

The Dixons are Bahá'ís. Eugene explained that it was the only place
he ever felt comfortable; where his interracial background—his father was
black, his mother white—was embraced. If I were religiously inclined, I
would be Bahá'í. For present purposes, I wanted Tom to meet the part of
my family that is remarkable for its beliefs and magnanimity.

ONE HUMAN RACE

One of the world's youngest independent religions, the Bahá'í faith espouses a core belief in the oneness of humanity and the need for unification of all nations into one global society. Men and women are equal, and the idea that any group of people is superior to another is anathema. Prejudices that breed contention and strife—based on race, ethnicity, nationality, class, gender, or religion—must be overcome for humanity to realize a peaceful and just society. "Abandoning Prejudice," on the Bahá'í website, expresses it like this: "The very diversity of the human race is, in fact, a means for creating a world based on unity rather than uniformity. It is not by the suppression of differences that we will arrive at unity, but rather by an increased awareness of and respect for the intrinsic value of each separate culture, and indeed, of each individual. It is not diversity itself which is the cause of conflict, but rather our immature attitude towards it, our intolerance and misconceptions of others."

Tom's Story

Lindi and I spent Thanksgiving with my daughter Emily and her family at their home in Portland, Oregon. Afterward, Lindi went home while I flew to Los Angeles, rented a car, and drove to my parents' apartment in San Dimas.

Mom asks me about Sharon.

"Where did you meet her? What's she like? Where's she from?"

I play coy. I don't want to instill preconceived notions. Sharon and I didn't talk in advance about whether to tell my family what we were doing so I just go with my instincts and keep quiet. They'll meet at my sister's tomorrow. We'll see what happens.

"Why don't you drive with us?" Mom asks. "It'll just be Dad and me and Aunt Net so there's room for the two of you."

"It would be pretty cramped with five of us in your car, Mom. Besides, we might want to leave Cindi's at different times. I'll pick Sharon up, and we'll meet you there."

God, I hope this isn't going to be awkward.

The next day, I pick Sharon up around noon for our two-hour drive to my sister's. California has changed so much since I lived here. More freeways, new routes, whole new cities; thank goodness for GPS.

During the ride, we talk about our families, Coming to the Table, and what we've each done over the past few days. The one comment Sharon makes that puzzles me comes after we turn off the highway onto a rural, curvy, sometimes-narrow road.

Sharon's Story

"What the hell am I doing?" I think to myself. This moment screams out against every admonition I ever received. Don't go where you don't understand exactly where you're going. Always have a plan of escape. Maintain control of every situation you can; especially when it involves white people.

Since we turned off the freeway, this country road looks like it leads to the middle of nowhere. We cross a small bridge over a creek on the narrow road that has darkened with the ever-thickening cover of trees.

"Is there another way out of here?" I ask.

Tom turns his head and glances at me with a quizzical look on his face. "What?"

"What if the creek floods and washes out that bridge? How do we get out of here?"

"I don't know. I can't imagine that happening. The sky is pretty blue. Is this your paranoia showing?" he jokes.

I don't think it's funny.

Tom's Story

My sister lives in north San Diego County, in an agricultural area dominated by lemon, orange, and avocado groves. My brother-in-law, Larry, has been in the business as long as I've known him. The population of Valley Center is predominately white. Black folks make up less than 1 percent.

I made light of Sharon's concern not out of disrespect. In my opinion, there was nothing to worry about. We're going to my sister's. This is my family. Sharon will be warmly welcomed. I would never harbor such fears . . . unless I was driving through Harlem.

When Lindi and I got married in 1986, our honeymoon plans included a visit with my distant cousin Halsey DeWolf Howe on Cape Cod. Meeting Halsey changed my life in ways I could not have imagined back then. He shared colorful, engaging stories long into the night about our mutual, long-dead relatives from Bristol, Rhode Island. Lindi and I added Bristol to our itinerary. Twenty years later, this meeting became the impetus for my introduction to Katrina Browne, another distant cousin. Without Halsey's influence, I would not have been part of *Traces of the Trade*, the film she made, or written *Inheriting the Trade*. I certainly would never have met Sharon Morgan.

The drive from Rhode Island took us through New York City. Way back in 1986, GPS had not been invented. There were no Google Maps or MapQuest. We used the ancient navigational tool of the day: a folded paper map. Lindi did her best to anticipate freeways we should stay on and when we would need to transfer onto a different one. I grew frustrated when we encountered highways she didn't see on the map and snapped at her more than once. Our progress was impeded by road construction in New York City.

I took what I thought was the proper exit. It wasn't. We found ourselves driving along a street in Harlem, gazing at the elevated freeway far above. Every building was encircled by a cyclone fence topped with razor wire. Heavy bars were visible in the windows. Crowds of people sat, stood, and walked about. None of them were white. A few stared as we passed. My heart was beating hard in my chest. I'm sure I snapped at Lindi again; wanting to blame her for our predicament.

"Don't be conspicuous," I whispered without looking at her, "but make sure your door is locked."

I didn't ask for directions. I just kept driving, block after block after block. I don't remember how we got back onto the freeway. I only remember the fear.

Sharon's Story

My son lives in Harlem. It is much like where I grew up in Bronzeville. I find it funny that it scared Tom. Maybe now he'll appreciate why I am afraid of being stranded in backabush California on the road to his sister's house, surrounded by white people, headed for a meeting with a white family I don't know and would not be part of my experience at all were it not for this crazy adventure we're on.

"You must understand how significant it is for me to trust you like this," I say. "My life is in your hands. A white man controls this car. You're driving me to a farm in the middle of God-knows-where for dinner with a bunch of who-knows-who white people."

"But it's just my family," says Tom. "Aunt Net is relatively harmless. You might want to watch out for my sister, though."

Tom's Story

I pull into Cindi and Larry's driveway not knowing what to expect. No one knows Sharon and I are writing a book together, so I doubt we'll be talking about race or Coming to the Table. Jeanette, my mother's sister, whom my cousins and I call "Aunt Net," answers the front door. Cindi, drying her hands on a towel, walks out from the kitchen to greet us.

My sister and I have had a complicated, somewhat competitive relationship all our lives. Since I moved to Oregon forty years ago, I haven't spent much time with her family. I've only been to her home twice before this weekend.

When we first arrive, I stick close to Sharon. She seems to enjoy Cindi's appetizers. I continue to glance in her direction from time to time, looking for any noticeable signs of uneasiness but she appears relaxed. Ignoring the ball game on TV, she and Aunt Net engage in a lively conversation. I have no idea what they're talking about, but they look comfortable. I hope that's true.

We snack. We talk. We joke. We watch football. We tease Aunt Net. My nephew Charlie and his wife Brooke arrive several hours late. We tease them. Charlie offers a blessing for the food. Plates and glasses are filled.

After pie and ice cream, Dad, Mom, and Aunt Net depart. Sharon and I leave soon after. I don't know what either of us expected, but I don't think this was it. What had we done? Nothing really. No heavy conversations. No awkward moments. It was like so many gatherings where you sit around a table, welcome a guest, and share a meal.

Sharon's Story

There is obvious sibling rivalry between Tom and his sister. She made several sarcastic comments about her "golden" brother in whose mouth butter would not melt (wink, wink). She excused her fallibilities by blaming Tom for being so perfect.

After hors d'ouerves—a tasty artichoke dip I tried to devour by myself—we enjoyed a delicious dinner. It wasn't quite the same menu I would have served with my family, but close. Our food would have been spicier and there would have been macaroni and cheese, collard greens, cornbread dressing inside the turkey, and yeast rolls. That was what we prepared at my cousin's two days ago.

Black people don't eat just anywhere. In all the places I have lived, people are particular about whose food they will consume. I think it has mostly to do with taste. White people, in my experience, don't like spicy food. In the restaurant I once owned in France, patrons sometimes recoiled when I told them their dish contained ginger, which is thought to be an aphrodisiac. I was blamed for the conception of more than a few babies. In England, I found few appetizing things to eat other than curry, which I hear is now the national dish. Cindi's food wasn't spicy enough for my taste, but it wasn't bad—not bad at all.

Tom's parents, Nancy and Laddie, were reserved but pleasant. His mom laughs a lot. Brother-in-law Larry kept walking in front of the TV, which I didn't mind, considering the game was between the University of Utah and Brigham Young. Nephew Danny impressed me with his tattoos. He has more than I do! Charlie and Brooke's devout Christian faith is notable. They attend church multiple times a week. Being on good behavior, I watched my potty mouth. Aunt Net was the charmer. She kept the conversation going throughout the football game, dinner, and after. I liked her *very* much.

In short, it was pretty ordinary. Although I felt some self-imposed discomfort, I didn't feel threatened. The worst part was enduring that damn football game. Realizing that Tom didn't prep his family about our project, I restrained myself from bringing up certain topics. Race never entered the discussion.

The next day, we tour Tom's childhood haunts.

He was born in Pomona and lived there until he was sixteen, when his family moved ten miles west to Glendora. Steep roads lead into the foothills of the San Gabriel Mountains above Glendora, where Western Christian High School once was.

"So much has changed," he says. "But this is where I attended high school. Racial tension in Pomona was supplanted by fundamentalist Christianity here."

"Interesting trade-off," I say.

"Yeah, that's one way to describe it."

We don't stay long. Tom drives down the hill, turns east on Foothill Boulevard, and takes us to Pomona. We park in front of the house where he grew up.

"When we moved here in the early 1960s, there were only two houses on this block. Mr. Jordan lived there." He points to the house next door. "He was the carpenter who built both of them."

He then points to the house next door on the other side. "Keith, Charlie, and Laura lived there. Billy and Mike lived on the other side of Mr. Jordan's house, and Mark and Janet were behind them, across the alley. God, there were a lot of kids on this block. We played hide-and-seek every summer night until our parents made us come inside. There was a big tree between the sidewalk and the street here. That was home base. I can't tell you how many times I counted to one hundred while my sister and our friends hid."

"Where did the black people live?" I ask.

"Back then? Just a few blocks that way, across Towne Avenue," he says, pointing west. He starts the car and we drive in that direction.

Tom's Story

When my family moved to Glendora in 1970, Pomona's population was less than 90,000. I'd guess it was 60 percent white, 30 percent Hispanic, and 10 percent black. Today, more than 160,000 people live here. Hispanic folks make up more than 60 percent. African American people number less than 10 percent.

The restaurants, stores, and malls of my youth have mostly been replaced by newer restaurants, stores, and malls. Henry's drive-in; Nellie's Italian; Alpha Beta grocery stores; Ruffings record store, where you could listen to an album before buying it; and the Ebell Club, where Mom forced me to take formal ballroom dance lessons, have all been replaced or significantly altered.

We drive by San Jose Elementary School. When I was a student there from 1959 to 1966, almost all my classmates were white. We see very few white children running around the playground today.

As Sharon and I slowly pass my old junior high, Palomares, I explain that it was my first school where a significant percentage of the student body had brown skin. I remember seriously troubled times. The Watts riots in central Los Angeles occurred in 1965. Things were still heated two years later, even thirty-five miles away here in Pomona. At one point, black students presented a list of demands, three of which stand out in my memory. They wanted the cafeteria to include foods from African culture. That seemed reasonable—anything to expand the limited food choices in the "caf" would be welcome. They also wanted Swahili to be offered in addition to French and Spanish. At the time, it was beyond me why anyone would want to learn Swahili. Finally, they wanted *The Adventures of Huckleberry Finn* removed from the library because one of the characters was named "Nigger Jim." I didn't think about the politics of the n-word but remember being puzzled. Jim is the hero! I wondered if the black kids had ever read the book.

Lots of fights erupted between black and white kids. They spilled off campus. At one point, there were so many black kids from Palomares rushing out after school to harass the white kids at Pomona High a few blocks away that school officials changed our schedules. High school students were released thirty minutes earlier than us so the white kids could get home safely. The Hell's Angels showed up that spring. For several days they patrolled, riding around and around Pomona High on their noisy bikes. It was a not-very-subtle warning to black students that if white kids continued to be bothered there would be serious consequences.

Our last stop for the day is Pomona First Christian Church. My parents married here in 1951. Mom works in the office part-time. We talk with her and one of the pastors, Julie Roberts-Fronk. They give us some tips for restaurants where we can have a late lunch. We make our way downtown, where we eat at a Mexican restaurant with great food and low prices. It is near the Fox Theater, one of my favorite childhood haunts, which is still standing.

Sharon's Story

I don't know a lot about California. My mother loved it. She tried many times to uproot herself from Chicago to make a new start on the West Coast. Over the years, she managed several extended visits, but never a permanent move.

When I was young, we visited almost every year. On one occasion, when I was a baby, we went by plane. The TWA flight was forced to make an emergency landing when I stopped breathing. I have a certificate that commemorates the occasion. As a teenager, we rode the El Capitan, an all-coach train operated by Santa Fe that plied the "super scenic" route to Los Angeles. The mountains were awe-inspiring to a child from the flat plains of Illinois.

Aunt Janet, my mother's younger sister, moved West with my grandmother when she was in her teens. (Though my grandparents had a solid marriage for thirty-seven years, they didn't always live together. Off and on, my grandfather lived in Chicago while my grandmother lived in California.) In 1955, at age eighteen, Janet married a young man she knew from Chicago who was stationed on a military base in Northern California. Janet bore two children there, including my cousin Renee. My Uncle Louie (her brother) chucked Chicago in the mid-sixties. A postal worker, he arranged for a transfer and headed west. Both Janet and Louie settled in Altadena, living within blocks of one another.

I thought what Tom said about the student demands was funny. We enjoy our spicy food more than the bland "white stuff." I took Swahili in college to connect with my African heritage. I read *Huckleberry Finn* because we were required to read books written by white people for white people; "Nigger Jim" was definitely problematic.

When we drive to San Dimas to pick up Tom's luggage for the change of venue to Pasadena, his father is home. We sit in the living room to chat for a few minutes. "Why did you move from Pomona to Glendora?" I ask.

He doesn't hesitate. "I wanted my family to be safe."

Part of me wants to dig deeper; to pry open a conversation about the role race played in his life and that of his beloved family. The unspoken part of wanting his family to be safe was "from black people." I don't re-act. Just like at Cindi's I keep my thoughts to myself.

Race is such an omnipresent fact of life for black people, you expect everyone to take the cue when you want to talk about it. White people apparently don't think about it, don't want to think about it, or don't know how to talk about it. Maybe they just don't see it as important be-cause their lives have never depended on the information exchange. That means, in conversations with white people, we are drawn into the denial game as well. We keep our mouths shut and our emotions in check.

After the brief visit, we begin the half-hour drive to my cousin's apart-ment in Pasadena. After Aunt Janet left her husband in 1959, she, Renee and her younger brother Kevin lived with us in Chicago. I consider her more like a sister than a first cousin. We used to call her "Tootie" after the Little Richard song "Tutti Frutti."

I loved Aunt Janet because, unlike my mother, she was easy to talk to. That might have been because she was closer to my age; just four-teen years separated us. And, she was adventurous! She taught me to get around Chicago on public transportation, taking me to areas outside of my community; places where many black people didn't go. Later, when I would visit her in California, we'd drive to Venice Beach in her VW bus. I remember the joy of rollerskating along the beach boardwalk in a bikini.

It was important for me that Tom experience my family just as they are; no pretenses for the white man. Renee wanted to make the best impres-sion, at the very least providing him with a bed to sleep in. I wanted him to sleep on the couch. I wanted him to appreciate that, no matter what lit-tle we may have, we always share. It is one of the lessons I learned growing up. There were times when we had to crowd together, sleep on floor pallets and make one-pot meals (mostly beans) stretch to feed the multitude. The few people I bring to my family are being introduced into a circle of trust and I find great beauty in that.

That is not what I felt in his environment.

I felt like the odd person out; although welcomed hospitably, I was not quite comfortable. While it was no fault of theirs—they did their best to put me at ease—I wouldn't have wanted to spend the night. I wouldn't choose to endure another football game between the white people of Utah or be surrounded by the white people of Valley Center. Tom's world is glaringly white. Mine is very black.

Tom doesn't see that. The Pollyanna in him makes him oblivious to the differences. I never let my guard down that much. I wouldn't want to be in a dark alley depending on Tom to protect me from a mugging. He would probably hand the mugger a flower and give him the peace sign.

Tom's Story

I wasn't sure what to expect. This was going to be quite different than Sharon visiting my family. We'd only spent a few hours sharing a meal, wine, conversation, and laughs at my sister's house. I was moving into Renee and Gene's home for several days. I wondered what they thought about a cousin they hadn't seen in some years bringing home a white stranger for the week.

When I walk in, I rest my suitcase and computer bag against the wall in the living room. Renee welcomes me with open arms and a big smile.

A wraparound sectional sofa—where I will sleep—allows lots of people to gather in the living room of the three-bedroom apartment. It was a good thing, too, because lots of people live here. Renee and Gene share one bedroom. Their daughter Dorothy shares her room with Sharon. Their son Josh, his wife Angela, and their small children, Elani and Aman, share the third bedroom. I also briefly meet Renee and Gene's youngest son Isfandiyar ("Fondi") and his girlfriend when they stop by to say farewell before heading north to where she attends school.

Gene and Josh are both computer guys. Gene recently lost his job of twelve years as a senior analyst with Kaiser Permanente. Josh works in the film industry, most recently on James Cameron's *Avatar*.

Angela, a musician, is the only other white person in the house besides me. I mention this not only because this is a journey about race, but also to note that Angela's being white in this family of people of color never came up in conversation.

Food preparation is hectic. With so many mouths to feed and all of us willing to chip in, space in the small kitchen is at a premium. We share delicious meals that Sharon coordinates. When she teaches Gene how to make gravy, a big smile of accomplishment grows on his face.

Two laptops are open on the dining room table; a third sits on a small desk nearby. Several of us peck away intermittently at our computers, checking e-mails and Facebook and sharing YouTube videos. An awkward moment unfolds when Josh pulls up "Being White," a clip from the 2008 Louis C. K. stand-up video *Chewed Up*, and says, "You gotta see this. He's hilarious."

We crowd around Josh's laptop to watch a short bit of Louis C. K. pointing out how lucky he is. He's young, healthy, and—he emphasizes—*white*. The audience (which I assume is mostly white people) bursts out laughing at this last point. Louis makes clear that he doesn't mean that white people are *better* than black people but that *being* white is *clearly* better. If given the choice, he would be white every time.

I glance at Gene, who is laughing out loud. Louis C. K. then mentions a key privilege for white people over black people: the use of time machines.

A black guy in a time machine is like, "Hey, anything before 1980, no thank you. . . . " But I can go to any time. The year 2? I don't even know what was happening then. But I know when I get there, "Welcome, we have a table right here for you, sir." "Thank you. It's lovely here in the year 2."

Of course, he makes clear, white people would only want to travel to the past. He doesn't want to think about what will happen to white people in the future when they are held accountable for all they've done to black people. The audience laughter is less boisterous at this point; a little uncomfortable perhaps?

Louis then points out that he's also a man, a *white man*—"How many advantages can one person have?" No kidding. This bit is really funny, and what he's saying is painfully true. I force myself to smile. I can't bring myself to laugh. I look from face to face at Renee, Josh, and Angela. They're all smiling or laughing. Sharon is laughing so hard, she's about to fall on the floor. This is one of those uncomfortable moments for many white people. When is it okay to laugh around black people or at humor directed at issues of race?

I know how much Sharon wants me to feel comfortable around her family, just like I want her to feel comfortable around mine. And I do, for the most part. The Dixons are wonderful. Yet moments like this remind me that both of us are entering worlds in which we haven't spent much time. It's just damned awkward sometimes. I hope that, by spending time in each other's worlds, it will become less awkward as we go along.

I spot Dr. Joy DeGruy Leary's *Post Traumatic Slave Syndrome* on a shelf in the living room—a book I've recently read. Joy (who now goes by her birth name, Joy DeGruy) is one of Renee's closest lifelong friends. Like the Dixons, many in the DeGruy family are devout members of the Bahá'í faith.

I've only personally known one Bahá'í believer before. His name is Chuck, and I worked with him at movie theaters in Central Oregon in the late 1970s. Chuck's heart was broken and his life devastated when his daughter was murdered by her boyfriend. But the first words I heard Chuck speak in reaction were words of compassion and forgiveness. I remember imagining how I would have responded if someone murdered one of my daughters. "Compassion" is not a word that came to mind. Connecting his response to his faith, I was startled and deeply moved.

I mention aloud my recollection that the famous '70s musicians Seals and Crofts were Bahá'í.

"Oh yes," Renee says, "We've met Jimmy and Dash. We have good friends who are close friends of theirs."

"No kidding?! I have all their albums."

It becomes clear that the Bahá'í world is a close-knit one.

Gene's sister Kathleen Cross comes over for dinner one evening to talk with Sharon and me. She is the author of two well-received novels and has appeared on *Oprah, Montel Williams,* and *Dr. Phil.*

Joy DeGruy's brother Oscar joins us the next evening. He is an actor who was featured on *The New Bill Cosby Show* in the early 1970s. Once a member of the Black Panthers, Oscar later started youth workshops based in the Bahá'í principles of equality, racial harmony, and unity.

A few nights later, Gene, Renee, Sharon, and I meet Oscar and his friend Janet in Los Angeles for dinner and a movie. We enjoy a delicious Cuban meal and then go to the cinema to see *The Blind Side* with Sandra Bullock. Even though this movie is controversial for many black people—once again portraying the noble white person as the savior of the needy black person—I feel comfortable. We've spent time together. We've shared meals and stories. It felt like we all enjoyed the movie. We laughed, and I think most of us probably shed a tear or two in the darkened theater.

We didn't talk about the film afterward, and the subject didn't come up the next day either. Was there no discussion because I was there? Did I not notice signals? Am I too sensitive about it now, overcomplicating it? Mostly, I just want to make sure I'm paying attention—something I never learned to do in connection with race—and not let my own "blind side" control me.

Another evening, Renee drives us to the other side of Los Angeles to the home of Walter and Barbara Heath for a Bahá'í gathering. Several other people are there when we arrive. We talk. We read Bahá'í scriptures. Walter sings; accompanying himself on guitar. He used to open for Seals and Crofts on occasion. Yeah, close-knit.

Walter is black. Barbara is white. Her family was not happy that she married a black man. Within the Bahá'í faith, it isn't an issue. Since my own journey began in 2001, I've encountered only two religious traditions for which I've developed strong respect due to their commitment to peace—Buddhist (at least as taught through the writings of Pema Chödrön) and Mennonite. This week I encounter a third.

As our week together concludes, it's obvious why Sharon wanted me to come here and why the Dixons agreed to her request.

CHAPTER FOUR

Lizard Brain

Sharon's Story

I moved to upstate New York in January 2010 for practical reasons. After losing my job and not finding a new source of income in Chicago, I packed up and headed east. My son Vincent was running for Congress in New York's 15th Congressional District; the one represented by the legendary Charles Rangel. I planned to work on his political campaign while I looked for project work. By living in the country, away from the hustle and bustle of city life, I envisioned time for reflection and writing, inspired by natural beauty and few distractions.

Tom is my first visitor. Our book proposal has been accepted by Beacon Press. Now, the *real* work begins. We plan to spend a week organizing our work plan and starting the arduous task of transforming our journey into a manuscript.

The first topic we grapple with is "Truth."

When I was growing up, there were few inviolate principles my family impressed on me. Telling the truth was at the top of the list. This could never, ever, be transgressed. I learned to believe in the truth as the safeguard of my sense of integrity and completeness. It is a principle I passed on to my son, who, I know, is passing it on to his children.

The truth was the truth and that was it—simple, exact, and easy to comprehend. You didn't play with it. You didn't exaggerate it. If you couldn't tell it straight out, you best not deny it. Your only recourse was to omit it and hope that your omission would never be uncovered. If you did something "bad" and didn't own up to it when confronted, that was "not telling the truth." If you embellished your stories with too much exaggeration, that was "playing with the truth." If you gossiped about somebody without fact-checking, that was "spreading a lie." If ever you had the temerity to utter a lie, you were guaranteed a "whoopin'."

My mother's older brother, Uncle Louie, once told me that truth was not what I thought but merely a record of "*his*-tory." Whoever writes the books gets to stake a claim for what is true or not, and until you write your own books, your story will never be told.

Tom's Story

Dr. Cheryl Talley is a regular guest professor for STAR (Strategies for Trauma Awareness & Resilience) whom I first met at the Coming to the Table gathering in 2006. Her presentation provided much for me to ponder regarding my conceptions of "truth."

Talley is an associate professor of psychology at James Madison University in Harrisonburg, Virginia—not far from EMU. As an African American and a woman in the study of neuroscience, she is a rarity in her field.

"It is understandable that people from different geographic locations, with different cultural and religious customs and experiences view the world differently. But what allows some people to view others as completely inferior? How can they possibly hold such beliefs to be true? What created the milieu four hundred years ago that allowed for slavery?" she asked rhetorically.

"Science contributed. Science claimed that white men have the biggest heads. It followed that they must have the biggest brains and thus are the smartest people. Science said black people needed white people.

"Religion contributed. Churches interpreted 'like with like' and utilized a few key scriptures to rationalize slavery.

"Law contributed. It is no accident that we are in Virginia. This was the first state to codify race laws, which dictated who could marry and who could own land. It is the combination of science, religion, and laws that creates a culture."

Talley displayed a three-dimensional view of the brain on the screen at the front of the room. She pointed out the oldest part, the *archipallium*, which she called the "lizard brain." It's located at the base of the skull. The key function of the lizard brain is self-protection; structures necessary for breathing, pumping blood, self-preservation, feeling fear, and so on are located there.

The *paleopallium*, or intermediate brain, rests above the brain stem. It comprises the structures of the limbic system and corresponds to the brain of inferior mammals. This is the "emotional" brain.

The *neopallium*, also known as the "rational" brain or neocortex, is situated at the top and to the front. It exists only in the brains of primates and, consequently, humans.

These three "biological computers" developed as life on earth evolved from the reptiles up through *Homo sapiens*. They are interconnected and yet retain specific functions.

"All instant responses to trauma are brainstem responses," Talley explained. "They are immediate and require no thought. This response becomes Truth; not my truth, but *the* Truth, deeply embedded in the lizard brain. These responses are very powerful. We share our story with those closest to us. Consequently, our children inherit the Truth. Much of what we 'believe' and 'know' are because of what others—parents, teachers, and society—tell us. They dictate how we see the world."

Talley noted that the brain is like a small universe. Neurons, which process our sensory or "learning" data, communicate with other neurons across synapses. When we do something over and over, it becomes learned like playing a particular song on the piano. Eventually it becomes fixed—an innate habit. We do it without thinking. Our beliefs about black people or white people reflect these same innate habits. We assume what we know is the Truth, but as Talley observed, "What each of us is raised to believe is the very thing that can strangle our search for truth."

"For example," she said, "Confederates in the South believed they had the Truth. If we want to reframe things, it's crucial to have a different response to our assumptions about the Truth. We know, for instance, that reptiles feed, mate, and fight. Humans also do these things, but possess the ability to use consciousness, gather information, and create wisdom. We need to learn how to calm the lizard. What you are trying to do through Coming to the Table is monumental. You are reframing centuries-old conversations."

To unlearn something as deeply embedded as racism or prejudice of any kind and replace it with new thought, we must first become conscious. Old thoughts are about feeling first and then thinking. Undoing such thoughts requires exactly the opposite.

"How do we get from being a victim to transcending?" Talley asks. "Change the brain. We need to stop living from 'lizard brain up' to living from 'consciousness down.' This is the new truth."

Dr. Talley's lessons dovetail perfectly with what Sharon and I learned in 2008 when we met for the first time. Coming to the Table feels like one of those places where the Truth can be questioned, examined, and reconsidered. It provides a "safe enough space" where people can talk about one of the most brutal episodes in world history and try to come to terms with it.

What Sharon and I have committed to doing is just that. Part of our journey, and yours, is to ask questions. In what ways did four centuries of trauma affect people, both black and white? What residue from that trauma has been passed on to us in the present day?

CALMING THE LIZARD

Psalms 85:10 contains the spiritual and philosophical foundation at the core of the STAR program: "Mercy and truth have met together. Justice and peace have kissed."

STAR provides the model that informs Coming to the Table. Growing from the ashes of the terrorist attacks of September 11, 2001, STAR began as a joint program of Church World Service and the Center for Justice and Peacebuilding at EMU. In the years since, religious and civil society leaders and caregivers from around the world have gathered at EMU for training. They learn effective ways to respond to the inevitable traumas of life that can lead individuals, communities, and societies toward healing and transformation instead of violence and war.

As we've seen many times throughout history, traumatic events— whether major natural disasters like Hurricane Katrina in 2005 and the devastating earthquake in Haiti in 2010, or human-caused horrors like the Holocaust of World War II—have the potential to awaken either the worst or the best in people.

Trauma takes many forms. For instance, individuals experience severe trauma as a result of physical, psychological, or verbal assault. Vicarious trauma may be experienced by family members, friends, victim advocates, first responders, or humanitarian aid workers. People who witness harm, who could have done something and didn't, may experience bystander- or witness-induced trauma. Participation-induced trauma is what those who inflict harm may experience. The impact on the oppressor can also be significant. Communities can experience collective or societal traumas as a result of genocide, war, slavery, and religious, gender, class, or racial oppression.

Trauma engulfs us where we are most vulnerable in body, mind, and spirit. It creates wounds that can affect us so profoundly that we may lose the ability to respond rationally, if at all. Chaos replaces order. Our experiences with each other underscore the dramatically different ways in which we view the world and the consequences of the historic trauma of race-based enslavement.

Resilience in the face of trauma is the ability to bend and not break; to experience a difficult situation, even trauma, and come back from it, often stronger. Yet we are often not resilient. For many reasons, we don't "just get over" trauma.

The legacy of slavery is a combination of historical, cultural, and structural trauma that continues to touch everyone in American society today. Historical trauma is passed on generationally when harm that happens to a group of people has not been addressed and repaired to the degree possible. Cultural trauma results when attempts are made to eradicate all or part of a culture or people. Structural trauma is inflicted when systems and laws maintain the injustices and inequities of the past.

Imagine the following scenarios as you contemplate the legacy of slavery and how it played out historically, culturally, and structurally, in the lives of individuals across the United States:

You are two years old. The only thing you are allowed to eat is cornmeal mush, doled out in a trough like food for a pig.
You are five years old. You have never worn shoes or clothing.
You are eight years old. Today is your first day working in the fields. You are expected to do the same work as an adult.

You are a thirteen-year-old girl. Your owner catches you in a field and forces you to have sex. He repeats his assault day after day until you become pregnant. Soon after giving birth you are required to return to work from "can to can't."

You are a fourteen-year-old boy. A wagon has come to fetch you from somewhere unknown. You will never see this place or your mother again.

These are the stories of slavery.

They don't end with the signing of the Emancipation Proclamation in 1863. The systematic dehumanization and disenfranchisement of African American people was perpetuated and enforced for another hundred years. Within our lifetimes, countless people have been traumatized, brutalized, and murdered—because of race. Even after the signing of the Civil Rights Act of 1964, the legacy continued.

How can we expect to face these issues with a calm, "consciousness down" approach instead of a smack-somebody-upside-the-head "lizard brain up" reaction?

Sharon's Story

I find it almost impossible to imagine reconciling with white people. At this point, I can only hope that this experiment with Tom will help me change my mind.

The transatlantic slave trade was a holocaust. It depopulated a continent, sundered families, and corrupted entire societies with tentacles that stretched around the globe. In the Americas, the enslavement of people of color was part and parcel of Europe's incursion into what they called a "New World." It was a world that was actually very old. The interlopers decimated the indigenous people who had lived in that world for millennia before their arrival. The oppression and terror were nonstop. The aftermath is something people continue to live with to this day. White people perpetrated more than one crime against humanity. Whether they accept it or not, their descendants continue to benefit from the bloodied rewards.

Despite my disillusionment and anger, I am still drawn to Coming to the Table and deeply committed to the work Tom and I are doing. There are some days when I don't feel hopeful about the outcome for myself, America, or the world. There are other days when I feel like David fighting Goliath. At least now, I have a kindred spirit to share the load.

Tom's Story

Sharon and I sit in her living room watching a DVD. It is a courtroom scene at the end of *A Time to Kill*, the movie based on John Grisham's novel. Sharon suggested we watch it—together. The protagonist, Jake Brigance, is an inexperienced white trial lawyer defending Carl Lee Hailey, a black man who has murdered two white men. The men raped and brutalized Carl's ten-year-old daughter, Tonya. When they failed to kill her by hanging, they threw her battered body off a bridge to finish her. Everyone knows Carl Lee is guilty. He shotgunned the perpetrators in the courthouse, knowing that in Mississippi, white men won't be punished for their crime.

In a wrenching closing argument, Jake asks the members of the jury to close their eyes. He recounts the crime in excruciating detail; imploring the jury to visualize the horror little Tonya endured at the hands of her attackers. The camera pans the faces of the jurors. Some cry. He has obviously struck a nerve. "Now imagine that Tonya is white."

That moment changes everything. It is a moment of connection; of the recognition of shared humanity between the jurors and a little black girl.

"You know this is based on a true story," Sharon says.

"Well, sort of," I reply. "I read how, when he was a lawyer, Grisham witnessed a twelve-year-old girl in a courtroom talk about being raped. He imagined what would happen if her father had killed the rapists."

"That child was raped!" Sharon cries out. She buries her face in her hands and sobs. She stands abruptly and rushes into the kitchen. I follow a few moments later to find her leaning over the sink. She is calmer but still crying. I rest my hand on her back. She turns and looks at me.

"It's been centuries of this sh*t. Don't you get it?" she asks.

She proceeds to tell me how her own mother was raped, which she says happened because she looked white. The perpetrators were black men, who did it knowing they could get away with it. They beat her mother unmercifully and then bought her father's silence.

We stand together in her kitchen for a long while without speaking. I'm certain Sharon's reaction is about much more than her mother's rape. It's the cumulative effect of "centuries of this sh*t." Realizing that, I still don't feel what Sharon does. I can't. I have no idea what it is like to be black. Her history, her experience, her inheritance, her anguish, and her education—particularly outside of school—are foreign to me. It's easy and natural for me to avoid comprehending the depth of communal despair and what it means to Sharon. I'm beginning to appreciate the reticence and flashes of emotion she sometimes expresses.

MONEY TRUMPS MORALS

The relationship between white people and people of color, in America and elsewhere in the world, has been built on manufactured images. White people came to believe they were the superior race and proceeded to convince everyone else of the veracity of their claim to hegemony. It was a claim rationalized by religious conviction, enforced with weapons of war and civil law. The newcomers meticulously built a social structure with themselves firmly atop a pyramid of wealth and power, systematically denigrating and disenfranchising everyone else.

Slavery has always existed, but in America it took on unprecedented proportions. The ability to acquire land and wealth was so immense as to be almost incomprehensible. The small bands of people who arrived on these shores from Europe could never have exploited the vast resources on their own. In order to fulfill their own unbridled avarice and the demand for products lusted after by the European market, the settlers of the New World required a labor force. The acquisition of wealth corrupted those who pursued it on the backs of others.

The story of the first Thanksgiving is of a multicultural affair. The Pilgrims were grateful to have survived their first year on a new continent. They were fully aware that they would not have done so without help from Native Americans. Indigenous people taught them how to adapt by cultivating crops and building houses suited to the environment. They generously provided much of the food for the first feast.

The Europeans repaid this generosity with a genocidal war that wiped out most of the Native American peoples of the New England coast. They established villages in the Northeast where shipbuilders and slavers plied their trades. They built tobacco, indigo, rice, and cotton plantations in the South, driven by the single goal of vast profits.

The labor to accomplish their climb up the ladder of success was stolen from people the Europeans came increasingly to see as inferior. The foundation of their wealth came at the expense of people locked into a pernicious system from which there was no escape. Humanity was snatched from people of color. The word "black" became synonymous with servitude. God's blessing was proclaimed on it all.

To say these events were deeply traumatic is a gross understatement. Not only the victims of slavery were dehumanized and denigrated; the people who traded, enslaved, and brutalized were also affected. The difference is that perpetrators were richly rewarded for their moral turpitude while victims were doomed to perpetual economic and social inequality. Anyone who fails to realize these facts of the American racial paradigm is engaged in a form of denial that is unfathomable to us.

ANCIENT WOUNDS

Racism is more subtle now than in the past, but it remains pervasive and persistent. Research in neuroscience shows that racial prejudice is rooted in the brain and emerged long ago (*Are We Born Racist?* provides a good background).[1] This prejudice has been inherited down through generations and still governs our instincts today.

This idea is taken further by Dr. Joy DeGruy in *Post Traumatic Slave Syndrome*. Her theory rests on the relatively new field of science called *epigenetics:* the study of the impact that life experiences and environmental conditions can have on human genetic code. The concept is that genes are altered by trauma and other life experiences and can be passed along to children and subsequent generations. According to DeGruy, many present-day negative perceptions, images, and behaviors regarding black people living in the United States "are in large part related to transgenerational adaptations associated with the past traumas of slavery and ongoing oppression."

To some scientists, this is heresy. Charles Darwin's theory of evolution—the general scientific view held since the mid-nineteenth century—argues against it. According to Darwin, DNA carries *all* of our genetic information. Nothing that individuals do or experience in their lifetime can alter the genes, nor can the impact of life experiences be passed along to their children biologically—just the unaltered DNA. Darwin published his conclusions in *On the Origin of the Species* in 1859. Yet, as Arthur Koestler notes in *The Case of the Midwife Toad*, half a century earlier, Jean-Baptiste Lamarck postulated that "adaptive changes in the parents were preserved by heredity and transmitted to their offspring." Lamarck theorized that animals and humans acquired certain traits as the result of their choices and their environment. Darwin's theory prevailed. Lamarck's ideas were considered a scientific blunder.

With the recent emergence of the field of epigenetics, scientists are reevaluating Lamarck's ideas. Epigenetics suggests that more than just DNA is passed to future generations. Epigenetics posits that powerful or traumatic experiences—nutrition, lifestyle choices, and other factors—can impact genetic "switches" and cause heritable effects in humans.[2] Scientists are coming around to the understanding that theories like Lamarck's and DeGruy's are, in fact, valid.

Scientific proof now exists that a powerful event we experience can impact the way our genes operate and can be inherited. In 2006, BBC Horizon released the documentary *The Ghost in Your Genes*. The film explores the hidden world that connects past and future generations in ways that conventional scientific wisdom never imagined possible. The documentary cites studies that have been done with Holocaust survivors and pregnant survivors of the 9/11 attacks. Results show that children can, in fact, inherit the impacts from trauma that their parents—and more distant ancestors—suffered. The imprints on our ancestors' genetic codes continue to live within us, even when we do not directly experience the same things they did. Further, events we are subjected to can affect our descendants. That implies an unbroken chain from the past to the future.

Sharon sometimes muses about our ancestors being with us, wanting us to find them in cemeteries, and guiding our thoughts and actions. She learned this concept in Africa. Ancestors are not really dead but part of a continuum of life. There is also an African concept of collectivity. People do not exist in a vacuum. What they do affects others and what others do affects them. Everyone is invested in and responsible for community welfare.

What we learned in STAR is that deeply traumatized societies exhibit terrifying social patterns. They collectively "act out" aggressively, and rates of domestic violence and other forms of abuse spiral. Gangs and organized crime flourish. Morality becomes flexible. There is a pervasive mistrust of people and institutions.

Does that sound like America today?

STAR explains this as a function of the "cycles of violence" we referred to in chapter 2. When trauma is inflicted, both the victim and the aggressor experience a range of responses. Victims experience physiological changes that can be detrimental to their health. They feel shock and anxiety. They often suppress their grief and fear. Conversely, they feel anger and rage and entertain fantasies of revenge. They may learn to feel and act helpless. They are hypervigilant. These are common trauma reactions initially, but over time, individuals and groups may get stuck there.

Aggressors, on the other hand, develop an increased sense of group identity and consciously decide to pursue their own needs, even at the expense of others. They dehumanize their victims as "the enemy," express an inordinate need for safety and justice and see violence as redemptive.

A victimized person can easily evolve into an aggressor, creating more or new victims, which in turn can provoke a counterattack against the original victim. The cycles can be repeated through individual lifetimes and passed on to future generations. It is this construct that must be dismantled in order for America to move forward in matters of race. Breaking out of the matrix takes a huge act of will.

Now, take a deep breath. When you finish reading the following paragraph, set this book down, close your eyes, and let your mind wander for a minute.

Think about the most traumatic thing that ever happened to you. Perhaps it was the death of a family member or close friend; maybe a difficult diagnosis from the doctor. Perhaps it involved a loved one's betrayal or the loss of a job. Whatever moment stands out as the most terrible, consider how it changed the way you think and the way you live. What did you feel? What did the experience make you want to do—and what did you actually do? Whom did you blame and who helped you get through it? What impact did it have on your relationships with others? How often do you still think about it and how do you think it altered your life's trajectory?

PART TWO

Shades of Gray

"But I suppose the most revolutionary act
one can engage in is . . . to tell the truth."

HOWARD ZINN
Marx in Soho: A Play on History

CHAPTER FIVE

Many Rivers to Cross

Tom's Story

I fly to Chicago in July 2010 to visit Sharon. Her world, though nearby, is quite different from the cloistered, university-protected Hyde Park neighborhood where I spoke at the Redemption of Reason conference two years ago.

She lives in a large, two-story, greystone townhouse built in 1884 in the original heart of Chicago's predominantly black South Side. The grave of Illinois Senator Stephen Douglas, who famously debated presidential rival Abraham Lincoln, is nearby. During the Civil War, it was the site of a training camp for Union soldiers and a prisoner-of-war camp for Confederate soldiers.

The morning after I arrive, I wake at five o'clock. The sounds of Chicago differ from those of Bend. Where I live, birds and wind chimes awaken me. Here, it is the din of traffic and construction. The stirring of neighbors announces that any attempt to continue sleeping will be futile.

We leave the house around 9:15. What I had done for her in Pomona, she will now do for me: introduce me to her childhood.

Sharon's Story

I'm excited to show Tom my hometown. Although I have lived all over the world, it is a truism that "there's no place like home." I grew up in

Chicago, went to school here, and lived here pretty much continuously until I got a passport.

When I grew up, black people lived in a self-contained section on the South Side. Today, it is called Bronzeville, which describes the color of its residents, acknowledges historic boundaries, and conveys the intention to attract tourists. The original name of the area was Grand Boulevard.

My grandparents lived on the street for which the community was named. Grand Boulevard was a main thoroughfare that led from south of downtown to the entrance of the massive Washington Park, created in 1870. Supported by wealthy patrons, the Washington Park Jockey Club sponsored racing, golf, and social events here from 1884 to 1905. The park entrance was embellished in 1902 with a statue of George Washington sitting erect on a magnificent horse, sword pointed to the sky. Black people lived in the area as early as 1890. I came to live here in 1953, when my parents split and my mother returned home to her parents.

I drive down the street in front of my grandfather's house and turn into the alley. I park behind the three-story apartment building where I grew up. It was once a brothel. My grandfather inherited it from a "girlfriend" who, like him, migrated from the South.

Tom sits transfixed as I describe the interior. There were mirrors adorning almost every wall: "Seriously, when you walked in the front door you faced a wall-sized mirror. To your right, a mirror hung on the guest closet door. You walked down a long hallway with more mirrors. We didn't have pictures; just mirrors. The hallway led to the dining room, where there was a mirrored buffet recessed into the wall. The mirror wasn't as tall as I was. I couldn't help but dip down to catch a glimpse of myself every time I passed by. It was my cousin Filura who pointed out that we all 'dipped' as we passed." I laugh out loud at the memory.

Sarah Pointer Lemon purchased the building in the 1920s. She furnished what was to become our four-bedroom apartment with Persian rugs, mahogany furniture, gold-plated dishes, crystal glassware, fine silver, and a baby grand piano. The piano was one of three made especially for the World's Columbian Exposition—also known as the Chicago World's Fair—of 1893. My grandfather played the boogie-woogie on that fine old instrument. I practiced my lessons on it when I was in elementary school. It was also self-playing. As children, our great pleasure was inserting the funny-looking paper rolls that governed its musical delights and watching the fingerless keys tap out their melodies.

The relationship between my grandfather and "Aunt Sarah" remains a mystery. She lived with us until the day she died in 1961, when I was ten years old. During all that time, she was bedridden. She left the house to my grandfather in her will.

Her bedroom was a magical place. It was furnished with—what else?—a mirrored bedroom set. Her closet held fur coats and glamorous silk and satin garments in which I loved to dress up. Her dresser drawers were a treasure trove of jewelry and wigs. I remember spending hours on end with the invalid old woman. I would go into her room, sit on her bed to read and talk and explore her marvelous possessions from another era. I have never been able to trace her genealogical trail, but her life was, no doubt, an interesting one. It certainly inspired my childish mind with grand fantasies.

After Aunt Sarah died, my grandmother immediately cleaned out all of her possessions. I was only able to salvage one cream-colored, oh-so-soft, satin dressing gown. It hung long to my ankles and was sensuously silky. I altered it to fit me. In my teens, I bought a complementary pair of house slippers. They had ostrich feathers on the instep and looked like something out of a *Frederick's of Hollywood* catalog. When I wore this outfit, I fantasized myself as the glamorous actress Lena Horne. I also saved one of Aunt Sarah's hats. It was a 1940s-style small, black "pancake" with a veil.

By 1930, the Grand Boulevard community was almost 95 percent black and was the epicenter of black life in Chicago. There were thriving black-owned businesses, active civic organizations, vibrant cultural institutions, and many large churches. We bought flowers at Kyle's Metropolitan Florist. People were buried from the Metropolitan Funeral Home. Most of the neighborhood residents bought their insurance from the Chicago Metropolitan Mutual Assurance Company. The wife of heavyweight boxing champion Joe Louis owned a wig shop on 47th Street. Black artists, writers, sports legends, politicians, and educators lived nearby. My grandparents or parents personally knew Joe Louis, the dancing Nicholas Brothers, dancer Sadie Bruce, songstress Dinah Washington, and comedian Redd Foxx. For many years, almost every famous black entertainer in America made an appearance at one time or another at the majestic Regal Theatre, diagonally across the street from our front door.

The historic Provident Hospital, site of the world's first open heart surgery performed by an African American surgeon, Dr. Daniel Hale Williams, was three blocks away. The *Chicago Defender*, the newspaper that exhorted black people to leave the South during the Great Migration, was printed in our neighborhood for more than fifty years. Its publisher, Robert Abbott, lived a block away. Anti-lynching crusader Ida B. Wells lived within a mile. Black children had role models all around, were exposed to lofty ideals about social progress and a visceral awareness of black achievement.

By the time I was born in 1951, all but a handful of Grand Boulevard residents were African American. Within its confines, people could be oblivious to the segregation imposed by "restrictive covenants" written into the Chicago Municipal Code that "forbade realtors to introduce members of any race or nationality into neighborhoods where their presence would damage property values."[1] My grandmother, a white woman, helped bust these redlining codes by purchasing property and reselling it to African Americans. Her partner in that venture, a black man, spent time in prison for facilitating the subterfuge.

The street on which I lived was rechristened Rev. Dr. Martin Luther King Jr. Boulevard in 1968, after riots gripped the city for a week subsequent to his assassination. Although we were proud of the name, we felt the change was merely a panacea to discourage further rioting.

In the early 1960s, almost everybody in my family lived in the same building. Uncle Louie, recently divorced and laid off from his job, lived in the basement apartment with his four kids. My mother and I lived with my grandparents on the third floor. Aunt Janet returned from California with her two children. Uncle Irving didn't live with us, but he visited often with his three daughters. An only child, I was in heaven with so many cousins around. All of us who were old enough attended the same elementary school: Corpus Christi, located less than one block from our front door.

Black people born in Chicago took great pride in having been delivered in the maternity ward of Provident Hospital. I worked there from

1975 to 1979. Provident was established in 1891 in response to denial of training and employment opportunities for black doctors and nurses and the difficulty black patients faced in being admitted to white hospitals. Many black people died for lack of proper care at major hospitals. If admitted at all, they were consigned to segregated wards in attics and basements. X-ray dosages were, for decades, calculated at higher levels for blacks than whites because it was thought that black people had stronger bones.

Many years after its founding, Provident deteriorated; people thought of it as a place to die. During my tenure, we fought a long and difficult battle to rebuild the then eighty-five-year-old facility and bring it up to a modern standard of care. In the midst of our fund-raising efforts, I asked the president of the Cook County Board of Commissioners (the body that approved financing for rebuilding hospitals) why he didn't want to give us the money to rebuild. I told him, "My mother needs this hospital because she is diabetic. When she is in crisis, she needs a nearby place to go. Wouldn't you make that possible if it was *your* mother?" He looked at me, shook his head, and supported our request.

I did not have much contact with white people growing up other than those in my family and those with whom I had to work. During the summer when I was thirteen, I worked in the Jewish-owned basement grocery store across the street from our house. The owner worked the butcher counter while I worked as cashier. I left when he started rubbing against me behind the counter, putting his hands in inappropriate places when I was stocking shelves, and making prurient remarks.

I wasn't sure if Tom was getting what he wanted out of this "other side" of Chicago tour or not. For me, it was a thought-provoking trip down memory lane.

Tom's Story

Through genealogical research, I discovered that I also have family ties to Chicago. In the midst of our tour of her childhood, Sharon drives us to Kimbark Avenue in Hyde Park to find the home of my great uncle Calvin DeWolf. All we find is a cul-de-sac where once there was a through road. Looking over the fence at the end of the now dead-end street, we see a giant parking lot where his house used to be.

"It would've been very nice," says Sharon. "As you can see, most of the houses in this area are mansions."

Disappointed, but not giving up, we drive to 47th Street, where Calvin's daughter once lived. Sharon gives me a funny glance when I tell her the address. Once again, the home no longer exists.

"This area has been all black for a very long time," Sharon says. "This is where the projects once stood."

Sharon's Story

I explain to Tom the unique role "projects" played in Chicago's version of segregation. When the Chicago Public Housing Authority was formed in 1927, its mandate was to improve people's lives by building subsidized housing for low-income families who were otherwise unable to obtain decent, safe, and sanitary accommodations within their income-paying abilities.

One of the first public housing developments in America was the Ida B. Wells Homes, located within walking distance of my family home. It was built in 1941, specifically to house African Americans who were red-lined out of other communities. The development was heralded as a landmark achievement in public housing; residents were hopeful aspirants to the middle class. But it couldn't hold everybody who wanted to live there.

The city responded with a master plan that concentrated public housing projects along a single corridor on the east side of a major freeway. Miles of public housing were built in a row on one continuous street. By the 1960s, more than twenty-eight 16-story buildings lined State Street, housing 27,000 people in 4,000 apartments. And that was just one section.

The western boundary of the projects was the Dan Ryan Expressway; part of the US National Defense System of roadways constructed during the Eisenhower administration. Buttressed on the eastern side by a railroad line, the expressway formed a barrier between the black and white sections of the South Side. In the 1970s, at the approximate midpoint of the housing queue, and right in the middle of the two boundaries, the city built a state-of-the-art police station.

"It was a common belief," I say to Tom, "that at any time the white people could block our escape from all directions, load us onto trains, and take us to concentration camps."

"What?!" says Tom.

I can see by the dumbfounded look on his face that he thinks I am nuts. "I'm serious," I say. Tom shakes his head and mumbles something about paranoia.

After that revelation, we make our way back to my childhood home and Corpus Christi, the Catholic elementary school I attended.

The school was three stories tall; the main entrance accessed through a serene courtyard, replete with statues of saints. In spring, flowers bloomed in abundance. This is where my graduation picture was taken. I am the tall girl in the last row, wearing a poufy pink dress and grey cat-eye glasses. The church is a Gothic masterpiece. The Stations of the Cross were rendered in oils around the walls. The vaulted ceiling made the marble altar where we took communion look even more immense and imposing than it was. Even now, my knees ache when I think about all the kneeling we did during daily Mass.

Catholic schools, perceived as vastly superior to public education, provided a welcome alternative for black parents. My mother, who had a limited education, was adamant that I should have a good one. She forced my stepfather to pay my tuition. It didn't matter that Catholics called her a "sinner" and told me she was going to hell because she was divorced. She never knew how the priest ogled our breasts and hugged the girls much too closely.

In fifth grade, I cofounded a "little nun's study club" with my two best friends. We all thought we might grow up and join a religious order. Our role model was Sister Mary Martin de Porres. The one black nun at our school, she was named for the only black saint we knew of at that time. Dressed in her black and white Franciscan habit with the peaked veil, she was both intimidating and inspiring.

By sixth grade, enraptured by the religious ritual of daily Mass, I succumbed to being baptized Catholic. An ancillary benefit of my piety was that my tuition was reduced substantially. That was appreciated by my stepfather, who remained reluctant to foot the bill.

I later sent my own child, Vincent, to Corpus Christi as well. His graduation photo was taken in the same courtyard as mine.

Directly across the street, I point out Liberty Baptist Church. Pastored for more than four decades by the Reverend Abraham Patterson Jackson, it is best known in my memories as a place where Rev. King spoke.

On August 31, 1966, King gave an impassioned speech from Liberty's pulpit that moved me deeply. I remember sitting there, riveted. His mellifluous voice, so eloquent and filled with emotion, inflamed my fifteen-year-old heart with passion for justice. I learned many years later that King was scheduled to return to Liberty in April 1968. He was assassinated in Memphis just weeks before.

As we continue driving around my neighborhood, I remark to Tom how odd it is to see white people. I can't help but gape when I see them riding bikes down King Drive, carrying tennis rackets to play on the courts in Washington Park, jogging along Oakwood Beach, and walking dogs. These scenes are disconcerting because they are new.

Chicago is one of the most segregated cities in America. Even today, although black people have pushed the boundaries and spread into the suburbs, in the city we remain divided into enclaves. Historically, we lived in an L-shaped swathe, concentrated on the West and South Sides. Where you lived depended on where your family disembarked from the trains of the Great Migration. Those trains transported millions of black people over several decades in the twentieth century from the prejudice and economic discrimination of the South to the promise of open housing and factory work in the North. Some 6.5 million people made that journey in two waves, first from 1916 to 1930 and then from 1940 to 1970.[2]

My maternal grandfather, Louis Nicholson, worked the train that brought many of them here. He labored with his brother Albert in the dining car of the *City of New Orleans*, the train immortalized in song by Arlo Guthrie. The train, operated by the Illinois Central Railroad Company, plied a route parallel to the Mississippi River from New Orleans through Mississippi and Tennessee. The line culminated at the 12th Street Station in Chicago, where black migrants from the South disembarked to begin their new lives on the South Side.

Until 1964, when the Civil Rights Act became law, this train, just like every other American train and bus in the South, was segregated. On the way north, Canton, Mississippi, was the changeover point where people could move from the colored cars and have open access to the bathrooms and dining car.

Louis Nicholson and his siblings departed for the north from West Point, Mississippi, soon after their father died in 1907. My paternal grandfather, Robert Leslie, came to Chicago from Alabama. I don't know how he got here, but I would bet it was on another Illinois Central train. He fled the South in search of work after his wife died, leaving three young sons behind. Julia, my grandmother, died in 1921 of pellagra. Caused by poor nutrition, this disease was a virtual epidemic in impoverished communities. After coming to Chicago as a child, my father never returned to his birthplace in Montgomery, not even for a short visit.

As Tom and I drive along, I can't help but think about how different our lives and histories are. Tom is like the white people I see walking in my neighborhood these days. It strikes me how they seem so secure, wherever they are. I'm pretty sure that it doesn't occur to them that something bad could happen or, if it does, they must have faith that the police will respond to their distress. In Chicago and places I frequent in the South, many black people still don't go to strange neighborhoods. The reasons have much to do with the long and odious history of black people being attacked—sometimes just for walking down the street. The famous Chicago riots of 1919 were caused by a black swimmer drifting into "white waters" in Lake Michigan. In 1961, riots broke out at Rainbow Beach as civil rights demonstrators staged a "wade-in." In 1992, the son of Chicago's mayor was among a group of teenagers who attacked a neighbor with a baseball bat. They were trying to evict two Filipino guests from a party at the family vacation home in Michigan. Although news reports downplayed the racial angle, our community was afire with the implications.

When I moved back to Chicago in 2003, there was an obvious drug market across the street from my house. Almost every weekend, there was a party and someone would get shot. Only when people died did the police come. My neighbors were afraid to call because the criminals would know who they were and target them for retaliation. What does one do in a case like that? I bought a shotgun and told the police I would defend myself if they didn't protect me. I then called every time there was a disturbance across the street, refusing to give my name. I also made a complaint to my alderwoman under a cloak of anonymity. It was she who spearheaded the removal of the drug market and made my life safer.

Shortly before I moved to New York, a white couple moved in next door. My black neighbors were abuzz with the news. I went to visit and welcome them. My black neighbors plied me with questions about what they were doing here and what kind of people they were. It turned out they were nice people. We visited each other often. They had decided to purchase a home in my area because of the attractive price. Their decision was taken against cautions by friends about living with black people. They told me they were repeatedly asked, "Aren't you afraid?"

Now that they are on the scene, I suspect others will follow and the neighborhood I know so well will be gentrified. I have mixed emotions about that. What will likely change is that the streets will be cleaned on a regular basis. The police will patrol more vigilantly. The schools will improve, and new businesses will open. Those are positive changes anyone would welcome. However, I am angry because they are things we as black people were never able to attract or count on. It's only happening because white people are moving in. My mother always dreamed our community would return to glory. It saddens me that she is not here to see it.

Tom's Story

I find the parallels in our lives interesting. Sharon thought of becoming a nun while I thought of becoming a minister. We both went to private, parochial schools. We both owned restaurants. The more time I spend with her, the more I realize how much we have in common.

The next day, we drive south of Chicago to the home of Sharon's Uncle Irving and Aunt June in suburban Lynwood. Irving Nicholson is the brother of Sharon's mom. He was a Chicago police officer for thirty years. In addition to his regular employment, he invested in properties that he fixed up and rented. He now serves as an elected trustee for the Village of Lynwood. He's the only one of four siblings still living. Irving and June Nicholson have been married for sixty years; they provide a powerful example of longevity, success, and commitment for their family. Sharon tells me he is the most economically successful person in her family and how ironic she thinks that is because he is the darkest-skinned of his siblings.

After introductions, the four of us sit in the living room. Glasses of wine are poured. Sharon pops back and forth, finishing dinner preparations that her aunt had begun. The aroma of grilled pork chops, collard greens, and other soul food dishes wafts from the kitchen. Our conversation is light, pleasant, and safe.

After we move to the dining room for dinner, Sharon tries to shift things. She wants to talk about the topic of our journey.

She asks her uncle, "How did racism affect your life?"

Sharon told me before we arrived how Irving, whose mother was white, felt the sting of discrimination due to his darker complexion.

"It didn't," he says, and looks to his right for corroboration. His wife nods in the affirmative. "I didn't let it. I just did what I needed to do to work around it."

I was surprised by his answer. It isn't that racism didn't impact him, I thought, it's that he overcame it. But the words and body language in response to Sharon's question said, "It was no big deal. We didn't *let* racism impact us. And that's all I have to say about this."

I thought that was the end of it. But several minutes later, without prompting from Sharon, Mr. Nicholson says, "The most painful experience I ever had was when I was a young man and my mother was in the hospital. She asked me not to visit because of this . . ." He rubs the skin on his arm and stares across the table at Sharon. He doesn't look at me.

It is obvious that the pain of that moment has stayed with Irving Nicholson throughout his life. The interesting thing to me is that he is a light-skinned man; it's just that his light skin is darker than others in his family. Talking to Sharon later, I ask if she thought the reason his mother didn't want her son to visit is because they would know she had African American children and would treat her differently.

"I don't know," she says thoughtfully.

Sharon's Story

I was the only child in the family who ever went with my grandmother to visit her family on their farm in Sidell, Illinois. I never thought about it until I was an adult and realized that was the case. I assume it was because I was the one who lived with her most of the time. As I think about what my uncle said, I doubt I would have been taken there if my skin were darker.

On our way back to my house after dinner with my aunt and uncle, I think about all I have shown Tom in Chicago. It feels like many markers of my life have disappeared. The hospital where I was born is gone, as is the hospital where my son was born. The high school from which I graduated no longer exists, nor the community college I attended. We no longer own our family house. The Regal is gone. My parents and grandparents are all dead.

I have a letter my grandfather wrote to my mother in 1945. She was in California with her mother and sister. The letter reads: "I miss you all very much. We are well, only very lonely for you." That's exactly how I feel sometimes.

Even though I was with my grandmothers much of the time, my mother's father was the rock in our family. Paw Paw was a strong but silent man who did so much for me just by being there. I spent most of my life growing up in his house. When he fell ill, he was the first person, other than my child, for whom I would do anything—including changing soiled diapers, which I did. When he passed away in 1974, I lost my anchor.

I never knew what his life before me was like until I traveled to his birthplace in Mississippi as an adult. Even worse than what I've lost in Chicago, the town he was born in has died. The train he worked on no longer stops at the Chicago terminal (which no longer exists) where he and my grandmother met. The steel mill where he and my two uncles worked is closed. Even the grave where he is buried is lost, along with that of my grandmother and many other relatives. Burr Oak Cemetery, one of only two inside Chicago city limits where black people were accepted for burial, has been desecrated—a scandal that became national news in 2009. Remains had been buried over others, or disinterred and dumped in mass graves. Emmett Till's casket was found in a garbage heap.

Tom's Story

Sharon is keeping us busy, that's for sure. We awake the next day and set out for a long drive. We're headed to Michigan for the weekend—to Three Rivers, where her Uncle Irving and Aunt June own a home that is used as a family retreat. But first we must stop for breakfast with Sharon's cousin David. His father and her mother were siblings.

"David and I used to be housemates," she says. Then she laughs. "He worries about me and wants to check you out to make sure you aren't the Boston Strangler!"

I laugh too at that one. If he only knew how many places we've already been; how much time we've spent together. We haven't killed each other yet. But I understand family concerns and look forward to meeting her protective cousin. When we arrive, David has already prepared a meal of eggs, bacon, toast, and fruit. We don't talk much; just eat our breakfast. Sharon and I are soon on our way. I guess I passed the test.

Sharon's Story

The house in Three Rivers is a big, old, wood-framed residence with six bedrooms. When my extended family is here for a party, we can be as many as fifty people. For those who sleep over, we occupy every possible sleeping space. Bodies litter bedrooms, closed-in porches, and sofas in the living room and den. It's like camping out indoors. At the end of the backyard flows the river; peaceful and calm and naturally filled with a variety of fish. Soon after arrival, there is a race to grab one of the poles my Aunt June thoughtfully stocks in quantity for these occasions. We head for the pier to try our luck at hooking dinner, and are seldom disappointed with the catch. Hands wait in the kitchen to clean and prep the fish, which are cooked in industrial-sized fryers and on outdoor grills.

When Tom and I arrive, we let ourselves into the house and unload our bags. What strikes me is how quiet the house is. Because it's just the two of us, it feels empty. No laughter fills the rooms; no jigsaw puzzles in progress on the card table; no raucous game of Uno; no kids running around; nobody fly fishing.

Over dinner, we jump into the brass tacks of the challenge that stands between and before us. I decide to push things a little further than we have so far.

"I like you, Tom," I say. "I think you're a good person. I hope this will continue to be a meaningful experience and I willingly welcome you as my friend. But I still have this thing in my head. I have great reservations about what all this is going to mean in the end. Some things about me will likely never change. My paranoia is probably never going to go away. I'm fifty-nine years old and the truth is I have a hard time trusting *anybody*, no matter what color they are. But I *really* can't trust white people. I look at the things going on around me and trust them less and less."

"I get that," Tom responds. "You and I have spent a lot of time together, and there's more to come. Here we are in this house in Michigan.

There's no one here but us. We've developed enough trust that we can stay under the same roof and you don't feel like I'm going to attack you and I don't feel like you're going to attack me."

I think about that for a moment. "So you and I become friends. What real difference does it make if it doesn't change our feelings about other people? How does it transfer into a more universal look at race relations?"

Tom pauses. "One challenge for me is that I partly understand but I also partly don't understand this deep mistrust you have of white people. I sort of get it when I think about all the horrific things that have been done by white people to people of color."

"But that's *exactly* it," I reply. "It's *because* of all the things that happened. I may never understand what it is about people of European descent that has made them tyrannize people throughout the world. What is it? Genetic? Psychological?"

Tom reaches for the open bottle of wine on the table. "Want to split what's left?"

"Sure," I say. He pours. I think we probably need some fuel to get this conversation rolling.

"Obviously," he says, "we're not going to figure out what drove people who are now dead. But there is stuff deep inside both of us. I yearn to understand and want reconciliation. I would like to enjoy normal relationships where two people can sit around, drink wine, and watch a movie together . . ."

" . . . and say whatever they want to say without feeling there's a pall over everything," I say. "We change our behavior when we're around people we don't trust because we don't know what they're going to do. No one has ever called me 'nigger.' I've read about many things that never happened to me. But I have seen things in the North *and* South that make it obvious those things are true."

Tom's Story

On the afternoon of our second day in Three Rivers, Sharon and I drive twenty miles north to Kalamazoo for dinner with my friends Donna and Al. Donna Odom is president of the Southwest Michigan Black Heritage Society. I flew to Kalamazoo in April 2010 to work with her to kick off a series of events designed to encourage community discussions in advance of the arrival of the interactive exhibit *RACE: Are We So Different?* at the Kalamazoo Valley Museum in October. The exhibit has been traveling to cities throughout the United States since 2007. With a focus on history and science, the RACE project explains the differences between people as well as the reality—and unreality—of "race."

That April, Donna, her husband, Al, Deborah Higgins, a program officer at the Fetzer Institute, and I met for dinner the evening I arrived. Al sat quietly while Deb, Donna, and I did all the talking.

"Do you ever run into people who are angry at you?" Deb asked.

"Sometimes," I replied, "not often. I witness anger and tears and long-standing frustration, particularly from black folks. But it isn't often directed at me. I believe it's directed more at the systems of injustice and inequity that continue to harm people. The more common response from people of color is that, finally, some white people are willing to speak honestly about these issues."

"What about white people?" asked Donna.

"It's funny," I replied. "Some of my cousins from *Traces of the Trade* were concerned that white supremacists would threaten us or something, but I've never experienced that. When I do presentations, the audiences are pretty much self-selecting. I've heard from many that seeing other white people speak the truth about racism, white privilege, and so on, sort of feels like it gives them permission to talk about it. It's liberating to acknowledge the truth and speak about it openly."

Al, who had been silent for a long time, finally spoke. "I have never heard a white man talk like you're talking." He laughed and shook his head.

I laughed too. "I see white men as my target audience. Throughout the past several centuries, the people in charge, the people with most of the power and money, the people with the most privilege, and the people who have caused most of the grief in the world are people who look like me: white men."

"That is the truth," Al sighed.

"Of course, that isn't how I pitched my book to the publisher," I said. "White men aren't the greatest readers in the world. Women are. But I figure that when their wives read *Inheriting the Trade*, they can turn to their husbands, smack them with my book, and say, 'Hey dummy, read this.'"

Al smiles broadly as he points first at me and then at himself. "You and me. FFL."

"Huh?" I asked, my brow furrowed.

"Friends for life."

I looked forward to introducing Sharon to Donna and Al, and they hit it off instantly. Donna prepared barbecued ribs, baked potatoes, salad, and bread, with blueberry pie and tea for dessert. Because Al and Donna hail from Sharon's hometown, the conversation focused a lot on Chicago. The three of them say, "You're kidding!" "I know right where that is!" and "Really!" a lot. I mostly listen and chuckle to myself.

The other day, when we were in Chicago and Sharon talked about her fear that white people could block off the exits from the projects and herd black people onto trains headed for concentration camps, I chalked it up to her paranoia. Sharon tells the story again over dinner. I know she's telling it on purpose because of the skeptical look I gave her when she told it to me the first time. Tonight, when she gets to the part about the trains and the concentration camps, Al says, "That's right."

There isn't much inflection in his voice, simply matter-of-fact agreement. I look from him to Sharon. She has a big "I told you so" look on her face.

"That's just crazy. What made people believe such things?" I ask.

Al says, "Just because you're paranoid doesn't mean someone isn't out to get you."

I'm reminded of Dr. Talley's discussion of deeply embedded truths. Rational or not, there it is.

Sharon's Story

The next day, back at Three Rivers, I remind Tom about one of our previous conversations. "You said something about all the 'isms'—racism, sexism—how they are all connected. They really are. You start stocking up these evil things that have happened and it makes you capable of doing evil things. It's a cycle that continues until somebody says 'I'm stepping off the wheel.'"

"So," says Tom, "if you trust one white guy, what does that do?"

I hesitate before answering. "I hope it enables me to be a little less guarded."

"And," observes Tom, "you say you never wanted to give relationships with white people a chance, but you agreed to attend a weeklong Coming to the Table seminar."

I laugh. "It's because I know there's something wrong and I don't always like the way I am. What we're doing is for the greater good. I also know it's not healthy to spend your life propelled by anxiety."

"As I was growing up," he says, "I think that one of the core things with me is that I really wanted everybody to like me. I've never had the feelings you describe. I tend to trust people first until they give me reason not to."

"With most people I think I do," I say. "But I expect white people to do something bad. I know we all need to be more open to honest conversations and to give each other some wiggle room without so much prejudgment. But what usually happens is that there are things we just don't talk about, at least with *you people*." I smile. "We rarely say what we think because it's probably not going to get through. So what's the point? We just kind of look at y'all and roll our eyes."

"And the walls stay in place," says Tom.

"I say things around you that I would *never* say around other white people," I say. "I told you I would do that. Here's something else I think about. Black people, we talk about race. It's almost daily conversation with us. There's always something going on connected to race. I guess there's no necessity for you to do that because you don't have to live your life on guard."

"That is a big difference between us," says Tom. "I just read Desmond Tutu's book *No Future Without Forgiveness*. He said the reason the system persists is with the acquiescence of people who are not in power but look like the people in power. We, meaning white people, go along because it serves us."

"That's absolutely true," I say. "The conspiracy of silence has become automatic. White people don't see how much they have benefited and get righteously indignant about the past. That's frightening. It's like in Nazi Germany. Did you read the book *The Reader*?"

"I watched the movie. I didn't read the book," says Tom.

"Then you remember the part where the German sentry was guarding Jewish prisoners. One night, there is a problem. The guards lock them inside a church to keep them from escaping. The church catches fire and the guards won't let them out—not even to save their lives—even as they hear their screams.

"When this guard's asked in court, 'Why did you allow them to burn to death?' she answers, 'Because if we would've let them out, there would have been chaos.' That's how people think. If we don't keep this established order, there will be chaos."

Tom tells me "One of the history people we met while filming *Traces of the Trade* said that everyone blames six million deaths on Hitler."

"He never killed anyone," we both say in unison.

"Not one person," I add. "It was average, everyday citizens that killed those people."

Tom completes the thought. "People lived in villages right next to the concentration camps and still claimed they didn't know anything. But they brought clothes and food in and out . . ."

Dinner is done; we have been lost in discussion over empty plates. We sit in silence. It is dark outside. Snapping back to reality, Tom stands and begins clearing the table. He says, "There are times when I'm not very hopeful at all . . . not on the large scale. What gives me hope are individual relationships. I don't care so much about laws changing if people's hearts aren't going to change."

CHAPTER SIX

The Past Is Present

Tom's Story

I often joke, when asked where I'm from, that I live in "Wonder Bread, Oregon." It's less funny when you cut away the crust and examine just how white the bread is.

According to the 2010 census, Oregon's population comprises 83.6 percent white people and 1.8 percent black people. This isn't surprising when you consider state history. Oregon is white by design. When the constitution was ratified in 1857, two issues were referred to voters. Asked whether Oregon should become a "free" or "slave" state; 75 percent voted against slavery. And 89 percent of voters agreed that free black people should be prohibited from immigrating here. Not one county came close to voting in favor of allowing free blacks in Oregon.[1] This provision remained in the state constitution until 1926.

Well into the 1970s, the effects of Oregon having once been a "sundown" state—one that is purposely all-white—were still being felt.[2] I've been told that laws prohibiting African American people from being within city limits after sundown were still on the books of some communities, including some in Central Oregon, where I have lived for many years. Between 1956 and the early 1970s, the black neighborhood in Portland—known as the Albina district—was systematically decimated as buildings were demolished to make way for a series of huge construction projects, including the Memorial Coliseum, Emmanuel Hospital, the Fremont Bridge, and the Interstate-5 freeway to Seattle.[3]

Recent census figures for the city of Bend indicate that 87.3 percent of residents are white and 0.4 percent are black. That's a significant change from ten years earlier, when 94 percent of the population was white and black people comprised only 0.2 percent.

When we talked on the telephone, as Sharon prepared to fly to Oregon to visit Lindi and me in September, I joked that the number of black people had doubled in the past decade.

"I bet you'll feel right at home!" I told her.

After seeing where Sharon grew up, I'm sure the wide-open spaces of Central Oregon will feel quite different to her. Deschutes County is two and a half times larger than the state of Rhode Island, more than 3,000 square miles. Seventy-five percent of the land is owned by the federal government. That provides a lot of room for playing outdoors, which we do regularly.

Sharon's Story

So here I am in Oregon, not a place in which I would find myself under normal circumstances. This experiment is the only thing that brings me here.

Tom fetches me at Roberts Field, the tri-county airport in Redmond. I arrive on a small plane with few passengers. I have no problem locating him in the eerily quiet terminal.

The drive into Bend takes half an hour on the Dalles-California Highway, a road that would take us to California if we kept going. You can see for miles in all directions, largely desert. The horizon is punctuated with massive volcanic mountains. From our vantage point on Highway 97, I am thankful that the last time these behemoths erupted was more than two thousand years ago. That means I should have a safe, grounded experience as I meet Tom's family.

Tom points out the Three Sisters mountains, dubbed Faith, Hope, and Charity by early settlers. "But no one calls them that anymore," he tells me. There is also Mount Bachelor and Three Fingered Jack (sounds like one of the sisters ran out of luck!). Tom explains that people come from all over the world to climb Smith Rocks, which also rises from the floor of the desert in the distance. This is something I always thought only white people do. I can't imagine clinging to a rock face for fun.

When we reach Bend, Tom turns into the street on which he lives. I am immediately impressed with the modest but attractive wooden houses. Tom explains that the area was developed as a community for people who worked in lumber mills.

"It was timber that fueled the economy that supported Bend's growth and provided the raw material out of which most of these houses are built," Tom tells me. "I was once told that a millworker could bring home whatever he could carry on his back. Based on the many different types and sizes of wood used to build our house back in the 1920s, that story sounds plausible."

The original houses were small and functional. Modern owners have built additions, painted them different colors, and added interesting artistic touches. Tom's next-door neighbors are installing aluminum sheeting on the outside walls. It is quite stunning, reflecting the changing light of the day. It doesn't rain while I am here, but I can easily imagine the soothing pitter-patter the rain will make. It is a far cry from the tin-roofed shacks I've seen where poor people live in Jamaica and Africa.

Tom's house is painted in vivid hues of purple and teal. A huge carving of a family of wolves dominates the front yard. Tom explains it was created by a chainsaw artist from the trunk of a ponderosa pine tree. There is also a colorful abundance of wildflowers. This is a home after my own heart.

My bedroom is comfortably appointed with a cushy bed and immediate access to a bathroom. It faces front, where I can see the cat every morning as he lolls in the sun on the porch, which ends up being my favorite spot.

Lindi DeWolf, like Tom, is blond and blue-eyed. Her pleasant disposition makes it easy for me to relax. During my visit, she teaches me to play Mah Jongg, something I always wanted to learn.

Tom tells me they float the Deschutes River with their friend Jane almost every day, weather permitting. They pack inflatable rafts on top of their car, head upriver, unload, jump in, and heave off. Since the weather is fine, this will be on the agenda while I'm here. I'm not quite sure I want to do this, though I love the water—sailing on Lake Michigan in Chicago and fishing in Three Rivers. Maybe I'm too urban or maybe it's because I am black. Urban black people I know don't raft on rivers or do things outside in the cold. We don't take off in the middle of the day to meander.

When the day arrives, I throw caution to the wind, help load the rafts, push off, and waft down the river. Lots of other people are jumping into kayaks, inner tubes, and rafts alongside us. Kids splash in the water near shore. We encounter ducks, geese, and swans along the way. This ends up being a truly pleasant experience.

Two additional highlights were our visit to the coast with Tom and Lindi's friends Brad and P.J., and a birthday party for their grandson Seth at Bullwinkle's Family Fun Center.

The coast is magnificent, very different from the Pacific frontage in Southern California, which I have visited many times. Because it is not so commercially developed, it reminds me of the Atlantic Ocean in Cameroun. There, I sat on the beach and contemplated how the waters that washed my feet in Africa carried black people across to America, where someone on the opposite shore awaited to sell them. Here, I merely marvel at the rough waters and huge dunes. I also note, once again, there are no other black people save me.

On the way back, we attended a birthday party at Bullwinkle's, a wonderland of climb-on things, games, laser tag, go-karts, and pizza. As a grandmother, I know the drill; Tom needs to fulfill family duties. I witness what that means for a white family in his part of the world. I meet Tom's ex-spouse, and all of their kids and grandkids. They appear to be one big happy family. Here too, I notice no black people. After cordial introductions, I sit on the sidelines and crochet.

My biggest impression about Oregon—which bears repeating—is how overwhelmingly white everything is. I noticed only three people of color during my entire one-week visit. That includes Bend, the Pacific Coast, and all points in between. I wonder whether this is intentional segregation or merely the effect of white people being in such a majority. I feel vaguely uncomfortable in being statistically irrelevant and realize there's great comfort in being with people who are the same as you.

I like being with black people. They are familiar. I feel safe in their presence, in spite of the horrific things we have been doing to one another lately. If a racially charged event were to occur in Bend, what would happen? I laugh to myself. There are not enough black people to pull off a demonstration of civil disobedience, much less a riot.

I wonder why white people seem so connected to nature. They hike, ski, climb mountains, camp out, hunt, fish, and find joy in living in dangerous environs—like being surrounded by volcanoes. Maybe it has something to do with being in control—of their environments as well as everything else. Maybe it's the urban person in me who grew up in a noisy city with little exposure to nature that makes me wonder.

I have a hunch that comfort is the key. White people feel safe wherever they are. I don't. I expect something bad to happen. I expect to be unprotected if something does happen. I expect to become a victim. I expect to be looked at, pointed out, and singled out—especially if I am the only black person in town. I expect to automatically be declared guilty if even one black person—as unrelated as that person may be to me—does anything that goes against the white norm. In choosing a place to live, Bend would not be on my list.

Tom's Story

Showing each other the places we grew up as well as the places we now call home was a brilliant idea on Sharon's part. Meeting each other's family and friends, participating in activities—even doing the mundane things—have all contributed to building trust and growing a connection with each other. There have been a few awkward moments, but I think we've both been pleased by how smoothly things have gone.

Sharon's Story

In November 2010, we spend some writing time at my house in New York and then embark on a road trip to Bristol, Rhode Island. I'm keen to see Linden Place, the historic home of the DeWolf family. Built in 1810 from slave-trading profits, it is now a museum that attracts thousands of visitors each year.

Bristol is the perfect next step after Bend. I now have enough information to make it worthwhile. Before going into the "belly of the beast" I needed to gain some comfort in my relationship with Tom. I was able to see Tom, Lindi, his children, grandchildren, and several of their friends in a modern way; absent the limitations impressed by history. I recognize that the DeWolfs are much like me. Except for the color of our cultures, they are ordinary people, living their lives in an ordinary way. We will travel to Bristol as equals. I know his history. He knows mine. We have built up a trust factor to carry us forward.

Our ancestors inform much of who we are. Many societies revere them for that very reason. They believe that death is not the end; ancestors continue to watch over us. An African proverb says: "You are not dead as long as someone remembers your name."

The DeWolf name is definitely one to be remembered. The family was responsible for importing at least ten thousand human beings from Africa into slavery. When James DeWolf died in 1837, he was reportedly the second-richest man in America. My story is different. My ancestors were slaves. No one will remember their names. They are representative of the people the DeWolfs collected and brought to America for sale.

Tom's Story

I've looked forward to showing Sharon around Bristol. Though I'm not from here, and no one in my line lived here, I feel connected to the place. I've come to know the town pretty well. I've done research, walked through cemeteries, eaten at restaurants, and attended church. I've grown several friendships here. Distant relatives continue to live in and near Bristol. Sharon and I will spend the night in the home of one of them. Helen Nadler and I became friends after we filmed portions of *Traces of the Trade* at her home. We watched President-elect Obama together on television in her living room as he spoke in Chicago after winning the election in 2008.

I drive Sharon to the cemetery where James DeWolf is buried. We visit the former DeWolf warehouse on Bristol Harbor; now an upscale restaurant named DeWolf Tavern. We walk into the Novel Idea bookstore, where Sue Woodman, the owner, greets us warmly. We eat sandwiches for lunch at Bristol Bagel Works down the street from the mansion.

I'm particularly glad to visit Linden Place while my cousin's artwork is on display. As part of the museum's bicentennial celebration, Elizabeth Sturges Llerena created an exhibit about the role of New England, Bristol, and Linden Place in slavery. She included watercolor paintings reflective of our time in Ghana, face-casts of people of color with quotes about their personal experiences of racism, and other pieces juxtaposed against the portraits and furnishings that are part of the permanent collection at Linden Place. The centerpiece is a dress called "What's Hidden Underneath." I wish the display had been permanent instead of being up for just three weeks.

I'm interested in Sharon's reaction. Since we entered the house she's quieter than normal.

Sharon's Story

Because I love old houses and history, I am enthralled by the magnificence of Linden Place and its surrounding gardens. The promotional brochure describes it as "the crown jewel of Bristol, Rhode Island's historic waterfront district . . . where generations of seafaring DeWolfs, Colts, and Barrymores entertained presidents and politicos." It says nothing about how they acquired their wealth or the people they enslaved.

In the garden, there are sculptures of fawns, nymphs, and other icons of opulence. The bedrooms are temples of elegance. Even the bathrooms are miracles of excess, with intricately tiled floors and mirrored walls. An ancient carriage in the coach house testifies to privilege. Tom tells me James DeWolf, a US senator, used to travel in it from Bristol to Washington when Congress was in session.

I wonder how moral people could live in such an ambience, fully aware that their wealth was produced from the abject subjugation of others. I doubt they ever contemplated that as they whiled away the afternoons in the gazebo.

I swallow my feelings and don't say much. I focus on the architecture and the furniture. I regard the portraits on the walls. I go into every room on every floor, including the uppermost one, which is blocked off with a rope across the stairs, so I can have a complete picture of what life was like for those on top of the social strata.

Because the entrance is through the gift shop on the side, I didn't see the dress in the front entrance until we were well into our tour. Tom's cousin constructed a beautiful colonial dress. It adorns a headless mannequin standing at the front door, blocking the exit. The outside of the dress is patterned with images of James DeWolf. In its abundantly folded skirt, the center of which is rendered in blood red cloth, lies a hideous secret. That secret is slavery; depicted with images of shackles, slave ships, and black faces. The artistic concept was both enormously creative and chilling.

After leaving Linden Place, we drive fifteen miles to Newport, where we stumble upon "God's Little Acre." We are so intrigued, we have to stop. Another case of ancestors calling?

God's Little Acre is located on Farewell Street; an appropriate street name for a cemetery. It is the largest repository of some of the oldest gravestones of free African Americans and slaves in United States. Two hundred eighty-five markers date back to the late 1600s. Some have descriptive information about the people buried beneath: names, places of origin in Africa, how they arrived in America. It is all there. I would only wish for that to be so at the many other cemeteries I frequent.

Tom's Story

I often think about the people who built Bristol. Experience and research have led me to understand how closely connected I am to them—even when I don't want to admit it. The oldest DeWolf ancestor of whom I'm aware is my nine-times-great grandfather, Balthazar D'Wolf, who shows up in the records in Hartford, Connecticut, in 1656. I have no idea where he was born; what nationality he was before coming here. His sons Edward and Stephen participated in the massacre of Wampanoag men, women, and children in New England during King Philip's War in 1675.

Edward's grandson Charles emigrated to Guadaloupe in the West Indies. Of his two sons, Simon, my ancestor, returned to Connecticut as a young lad to be raised by his grandfather. His younger brother Mark Anthony remained in Guadaloupe until 1744, when he sailed to Bristol and became the DeWolf family's first slave trader.

My line—Simon's descendants—were carpenters, hatters, and farmers. They migrated from Connecticut to Pennsylvania to Illinois to Iowa. My three-times-great uncle, Calvin DeWolf, was an influential abolitionist in Chicago. My father was born in Iowa on a farm that remains in family ownership today. The more I travel, the more I research, the more I discover people I'm related to.

I've heard that, if you can trace your family roots back to the seventeenth century in this country, it is likely you'll find African or American

Indian ancestors. My curiosity led me to take a DNA test to see if I had that "one drop" of color anywhere. Well, I'm 97 percent white guy and 3 percent Asian. I'm mystified about where that Asian "drop" enters the picture.

As we continue our journey, I wonder if Sharon and I will find any shared ancestry or other historical connection.

Sharon's Story

I have no idea whether there is an ancestral connection between me and Tom. His ancestors voyaged to Africa and captured and enslaved people. Were my ancestors victims of his? The ancestral voices inside my head say that just *might* be so. Why else would two modern people from different sides of America and divergent cultures be brought to the same place at the same time and moved in the same direction? Karma? Coincidence?

It would not surprise me at all if one day Tom and I discover some remote historical connection. His slave-trading ancestors operated long beyond the legal limit for importation of slaves. One of my ancestors was proven through DNA testing to have come through a gateway in Eastern Africa. Trade from this area was common once the law went into effect. What if an ancestor of mine was brought on a ship owned or captained by a DeWolf?

Studying genealogy makes me painfully aware of the absolute horror of all that slavery was. The pathos emerges vividly through on-the-ground research. When I started researching my family, it almost instantly became an obsession. In confirming slaves on *both* sides of my family, I was filled with horror and sorrow. With every name I uncovered, I yearned to put flesh on the bones of people who made me but were now long dead. I read everything I could find.

I wonder about my ancestors who lived before 1870, the year the federal census first listed black people by surname. Duties for female slaves often included "servicing" the sexual needs of their masters. Black men were studded out to produce babies. Children were put to work at four years of age and sold away by age ten. Families were broken up. People were willed to relatives and sold to pay debts. I think about the lost ones— brothers, sisters, parents, cousins—where are they? What were their lives like? Where are their descendants? What part of them is in me?

The maternal side of my family descends from a man named Robert Lewis Gavin of Noxubee County, Mississippi. Born in 1838, he was a teacher. His Scottish ancestors, likely fleeing religious persecution, boarded a boat headed to the land of opportunity. They arrived in America in 1695. Fighting in the American wars of Revolution and 1812 entitled them to land grants in the Carolinas that put their feet on the road to prosperity.

In the early 1800s, when the western frontier opened up for settlement, several Gavins migrated to Mississippi. The lyrical-sounding Treaty of Dancing Rabbit Creek, which forced the native population to cede their lands, made their move possible. Gavins owned slaves in South Carolina, Florida, Alabama, and Mississippi. The total in Mississippi was more than 125 people.

In 1849, a small girl named Bettie was taken from her mother. She was transported by a man named John Warf, who embarked from Virginia. He arrived in Noxubee County, Mississippi, with five slaves, including Bettie, who was nine years old.

Testifying in 1901 in a Dawes Commission case, Bettie was asked how she got to Mississippi. She said, "I came with some white folks."

"How did white folks have possession of you?"

"They took me from my mother."

The judge asked, "Did the people you were with consider you as a slave?"

"No, not that I know of; I have never been treated as a slave. . . . I have been with the white people all my life. . . . I have been staying with first one and then another."[4]

Sometime before 1860, Warf sold Bettie to the Gavins. The story that was passed down through my family is that he traded her for a horse. A tax record in Carthage, Mississippi, shows that he owned a buggy and a piano. I wonder if he hitched the horse he got in trade for Bettie to the buggy and drove it to Canton, where he acquired a plantation named Starvation Hill.

Nine years after arriving in Mississippi, Bettie gave birth for the first time. Her baby was fathered by Robert Lewis Gavin, the nephew of her next owner after Warf. She had two more children before the Civil War ended, and a total of seventeen. Given the conditions of the time, Bettie was fortunate that all her children had the same father and that most of them survived. It appears Bettie and Robert had a meaningful relationship; it endured for thirty-seven years. In another testimony, when asked why she was not married to him she said, "Because the law would not allow it."

As the great-great-granddaughter of Robert and Bettie, I struggle to comprehend their relationship. It seems they were devoted to each other but were forbidden by law from marrying. It would have been illegal for them to even live under the same roof, married or not. I wonder how meaningful a relationship could possibly be with such a disparity in the power construct.

Compared with the difficulties of tracking down Bettie's story, the challenge of researching my father's family was even more daunting. When I first expressed an interest in genealogy, my father was appalled. Nobody in my family talked about slavery out loud. My father adamantly refused to tell me anything. He said he didn't want me trying to search back to Africa. My thought is that there was shame associated with that connection. Slaves were indoctrinated to believe that "saltwater" (African) slaves and those born in America were different. Enslaved black people born in America were "civilized." Black people fresh from Africa were disparaged as "savages."

My father eventually relented and admitted that his grandparents were slaves. I met one of them, my great-grandmother Rhoda, who came to Chicago in 1939 after her husband died. When she passed away at 104 years of age, I was three. I remember her as a very tall woman who smoked cigars.

By 2003, I had traveled around the world. I had spent ten years living in South Africa and France. During those years, many genealogical records became available online that enabled me to make progress in my research even though I was overseas. When I returned to the United States to care for my ailing mother, I arrived armed with a collection of documents that hinted at whom the slaveholders of my ancestors were. I began visiting locations where they were enslaved. During excursions to Alabama and Mississippi, I saw how people who shared my genes had been harmed by prejudice and oppression. Even though many genealogical finds caused a rush of anger, I still found some peace in the knowing.

Additional pieces of my puzzle were discovered by accident. On my mother's side—the Gavins—I found several people who were genetically related but had never lived as African Americans. Their grandparents transformed themselves from black to white on a path from Mississippi to Chicago. Those who "passed" did so after being driven out of Mississippi. White or Native American in appearance, they left under the threat of being treated "like the niggers you are" soon after their white father died in 1896. Estate records documented Robert Gavin as a "bachelor with no heirs." His white relatives claimed the sixty-six acres of land left to him by his father. The court declared him a "lifelong tenant," which carried no right of inheritance.

Tom's Story

In the summer of 2002, I embarked on what I dubbed "the Dead DeWolf Cemetery Tour." Over the course of two weeks, I visited homesteads, farms, courthouses, city halls, libraries, and lots of cemeteries in Minnesota, Iowa, Illinois, Pennsylvania, and Connecticut. I drove hundreds of miles to visit the graves of cousins, aunts, uncles, and grandparents from the recent past all the way back to old Edward DeWolf, who died in 1710. His headstone in Connecticut is still legible after more than three hundred years.

The first relative I met was my father's cousin Phyllis Thompson in southern Minnesota. She showed me a scrapbook assembled over many decades. It bulges with photos and newspaper articles about our relatives, clippings from weddings, obituaries, birth announcements, letters, school report cards, graduation notices, and wedding and anniversary invitations.

Upon reaching the town of Rolfe, Iowa, I drove to the site of the long-gone farmhouse where my father and aunts were born. I imagined my aunts riding ponies, my grandmother behind the counter of the diner she operated downtown, and her and my grandfather on their wedding day. I looked out at fields of tall corn gently rippling in the warm summer breeze. I felt a visceral connection to the land, to the dirt on which I stood. I picked up a handful and let it sift through my fingers.

I walked up the railroad track to where it intersects the fence that separated my grandparents' farm from that of my great-grandparents. It was near here that my namesake grandfather took his own life when my father was two years old. I can't help thinking, if he hadn't pulled that trigger, my parents never would have met. I never would have been born. What does a person think about just before killing himself?

I also wonder if my grandfather ever encountered black people in his life. It wouldn't surprise me if the answer is no. I didn't see anyone of African descent in Rolfe in 2002, and my grandfather died in 1931. I think about the impact such racial isolation has on the worldview of people in such situations and that of their descendants.

I drove into town to the now-empty site of the former Presbyterian church, the one from which my grandfather and his family were "dismissed"—I've never learned why they were kicked out. I passed St. Paul's Lutheran Church, which they subsequently joined. I drove to the cemetery; a peaceful resting place with tall oak trees that provided magnificent cover for the graves below. I stood in front of the small headstone of my grandfather, who is buried far from most other members of his family. I placed a small bouquet of bright flowers on his grave.

Sharon's Story

Most genealogists consider graveyards sacred. They are repositories not just of bodies, but memories. When you locate the grave of an ancestor for whom you have been diligently searching for a long time, there is a rush of excitement. More than a sense of accomplishment for solving the genealogical puzzle, you feel a presence—the spirit of the person. It is as though your ancestors want you to find them; want to be connected. Many a ghost story has been written about cemetery encounters with those who passed over. The more time I spend with long-buried ancestors, the more I believe these stories are true.

Tom's Story

The first cemetery Sharon and I visited together was Oak Woods in Chicago; the most significant on Chicago's South Side. A mass grave known as "Confederate Mound" holds six thousand Confederate soldiers who died in nearby Camp Douglas.

We went to find the grave of my great uncle Calvin DeWolf. I don't have the mixed feelings about him that I have about the slave traders in New England; Calvin is a guy I can relate to. He was a fervent abolitionist. In 1839, he helped found the Anti-Slavery Society of Illinois and served as its first secretary. After becoming a lawyer in 1854, he was elected as one of Chicago's six justices of the peace.

The DeWolf home in Chicago was an active station on the Underground Railroad. Calvin once arranged for a Southern slave-owner who was in Chicago pursuing his "property" to be arrested. Calvin sentenced the man to several nights in jail, which allowed the black female fugitive he sought to escape. In 1860, Calvin was indicted for abusing his position. He was charged with aiding and abetting the escape of a fugitive slave. The indictment was dropped shortly after Lincoln's election in late 1861.

Sharon and I found his grave not far from Confederate Mound. It was near the gravesites of Chicago's first African American mayor, Harold Washington, and the once-enslaved, anti-lynching and women's rights crusader Ida B. Wells-Barnett.

As we stood at Calvin's grave, I explained to Sharon that the abolitionist was from *my* line. I admit that having Calvin in my family tree is comforting. Logically, it doesn't make any sense. I'm no more responsible for his actions than I am for those of the slave-traders. But we do tend to highlight the family heroes and hide the heels in the closet.

Sharon's Story

All the people directly involved in slavery are now dead. Yet the legacy remains. In spite of social gains African Americans have achieved in my lifetime, I continue to be reminded of this legacy every day, especially when I visit cemeteries.

Funerals are a big deal in African American communities. During slavery times, there was no ceremony attached to the death of a loved one. People were wrapped in a sheet (maybe) and tossed into the ground. Everybody went back to work.

Some years ago, I found a neglected cemetery in Lowndes County, Alabama, located on a property once owned by Dr. John Marrast, one of the largest slaveholders in the county. In 1855, he owned 128 people. I believe at least four of my ancestors were his chattel.

I discovered the cemetery on a satellite map. For years, I tried to find its exact location. I drove all over Lowndes County looking for a sign. There were none. GPS finally led me there. The state of disrepair made it obvious this was a black cemetery, one set aside for slaves. White cemeteries tend to be well kept, with lots of readable headstones.

My first visit to the property was frustrated by a locked gate, through which I feared to trespass. I searched for the owners and contacted them by mail, providing particulars of what I was looking for. Cattle ranchers who live in Florida, the owners had no idea there was a cemetery on their property. When I told them, they located it, cleared the land, and tied a red ribbon on the tree marking the site. They escorted me and welcomed me to come back any time. Sadly, there was only one intact gravestone; not belonging to any one of my ancestors.

I envy Tom having access to so many physical records that trace his family back to the 1600s. He can find gravestones that are three hundred years old. The trail for black people typically stops at the brick wall of 1870. That makes me profoundly sad.

Tom's Story

I recall the day in Tobago when Sharon was in tears as she read through a sheaf of papers Professor Lynch keeps at a desk near the front door. The papers were slave schedules that document the name, color, age, place of origin, and occupation of the people enslaved on Richmond Estate.

"At least here," she had said, shaking her head, "people were recorded by name rather than cross-hatches. And you also get to see what jobs they were responsible for. There are even notes on some that indicate their parents. In American records, slave owners kept more detailed records of their horses and cows than they did of the people they owned."

Later that day, Sharon was skimming through historic volumes from the eighteenth century about slavery in the West Indies. Once again, tears welled up in her eyes. It is so rare to see Sharon cry that it was really disturbing. Her voice rose with every sentence. "Whenever I read history—anything to do with slavery—even if it's not my own ancestors, I get so pissed off. Everywhere Europeans went, they killed everybody off, snatched their land, and proceeded to convert it to their financial benefit. Chattel slavery, as horrific as it was, was only a part of a much bigger picture. They renamed everything and then emplaced a system that reflected *their* values, *their* needs."

Her voice continued to rise.

"Can you imagine being dragged away from your home and brought to some foreign place to be worked to death for the benefit of some smarmy little Englishman who paid five dollars an acre for some stolen land and less than a hundred dollars for your body and soul?"

By then, she was almost screaming; pounding the table with her fist.

"*Stolen* land! *Stolen* people! *Murder!* If there is a God and he condones retribution, the white race owes a sh*tload!"

"I'm sorry, Tom," Sharon apologized a short time later. Her voice had returned to normal. "Even though I am committed to this project, I just can't help myself sometimes. Injustice piled on injustice piled on injustice, over and over again, century after century, all over the world. I know we have to move on, but damn! It is *hard*—harder than anything I have ever tried to do."

CHAPTER SEVEN

Colored Water

Sharon's Story

In May 2011, I attended the National Genealogical Society conference in Charleston, South Carolina. I spent a week working the Coming to the Table exhibit booth with my colleague, David Pettee. As the crowd in the exhibit hall ebbed and flowed, there was quite a bit of downtime, plenty of opportunity for thought and reflection.

One thing that impresses me when I attend genealogy conferences is witnessing how many people are seriously interested in the subject. More than two thousand people took the time to attend this one. Judging from the license plates in the car lot, they came from far and wide. Like me. I drove more than eight hundred and fifty miles to be there.

Our goal with the exhibit booth was to attract genealogy buffs who might be interested in linking descendants of people who were enslaved with descendants of the people who enslaved them. Well . . . it sure was interesting to see how people reacted to *that* proposition.

Our location as the last booth in the exhibit maze made it so everybody had to pass us if they circuited the hall. Many gave us a wide berth when they read our display poster (featuring a quotation by Rev. Martin Luther King Jr.). Others stood back and watched from across the aisle. We could tell that many people were curious, but they would only go so far—not far enough to be engaged.

We thought maybe our book display or the DVDs we were showing might be a deterrent. In our best attempt to be truly "white-people friendly," we rearranged the books and switched DVDs. That still didn't work.

I started reaching out to put information cards into people's hands. "Can I please give you one of these?" I repeated to each passerby. Although nobody refused, most wouldn't budge into a conversation. But a few did, and those exchanges were most revealing.

Those who wanted to talk were candid. I spoke with white people who had done a lot of research, knew exactly what their family history was, acknowledged the slavery aspect, and seemed genuinely interested in doing something—like making their records available to help black people find their ancestors. I also spoke with black people, mostly women, who ran into that standard 1870 brick wall blocking their research path. Many of these ladies wanted connections and were happy to discover a new resource.

Then there were the miscreants. One woman said, "Aren't you glad we brought you over from Africa?" When I said "no" and told her why, she launched into a diatribe about how black people were responsible for slavery because "they sold their brothers." What I said about the slave trade depopulating Africa and inhibiting its development ever since passed right over her head. Another woman whose caustic comments about "those people" in comparing "good" versus "bad" immigrants (read: "hardworking Mexicans" versus "fence jumpers") made my stomach turn. She wanted the bad ones sent packing (or otherwise "disposed" of). Was I supposed to feel all right that she said this in my presence and surely thought I would agree with her?

Although I am committed to the work I do, I get tired, angry, and resentful about the historical and emotional dynamic that compels me to be kind and understanding on the issue of slavery and other historical truths, even when it is clear white people are not. I had to really stretch myself to not respond in an aggressively negative way to the woman who thinks we should rejoice over being "rescued" from Africa. What I felt like doing was slapping her in the mouth. David stepped in and got me off the hook. In the end, I swallowed my ire and chalked it up to the blissful ignorance that American history books and society-sanctioned denial has made possible for people like her.

On the other hand, I am impressed by black people who are generally retrospective and compassionate. Many of us want to heal. Few white people seem to comprehend that healing is in order. How will we ever break through that psychological barrier?

My final takeaway is that it is a lot harder for white people to deal with the issues of slavery and racism than it is for black people. Black people have been talking to each other about this incessantly all my life. We need to see white people being serious and talking about it too. If they don't come together at the table, finding resolution is a lost cause.

Tom's Story

One of the biggest challenges we face as a society is encapsulated in Sharon's experience at the conference. Most white people want nothing to do with this conversation. Many of us don't know what to say. We don't want to sound stupid or say the wrong thing. Most of our friends and family also don't want—or don't know how—to delve into what we fear is a boiling cauldron of controversy. We weren't raised having these conversations except in mostly superficial and safe ways ("Everyone is equal . . . " "You shouldn't discriminate . . . " "Red and yellow, black and white, they are precious in His sight . . . ") so we avoid them. Other white people have strong opinions, are not shy about sharing them, and have no interest or skill in listening to anyone who challenges their beliefs.

My focus has been on impacting the attitudes and actions of white men. We've had most of the power and privilege, and have been responsible for the vast majority of oppression and injustice in the world for many centuries. Sometimes women drag their husbands to my talks, God bless 'em.

One time, when I invited comments and questions from the audience at the end of my presentation, an elderly gentleman said, "I'm tired of all this. You know that everything is a lot better than it used to be." His arms were crossed over his chest. His jaw was set.

"You're right," I replied. "Many things have improved over the past fifty years. The fact that black and white people can sit together in a room like this would not have happened when you were in high school. But we still have a long way to go before things are equal and fair."

"No," he said, "anyone can do anything they want in this country if they're willing to work hard."

A woman of color sitting not far from him leaned forward and shook her head. "With all due respect, sir," I said, "have you had a conversation about this with a person of color?"

He shook his head dismissively and didn't say anything more.

That guy represents the challenge. He's firm in his beliefs and is probably well-meaning for the most part. How do you engage such a man? If I had continued to force my opinions on him, it would have accomplished nothing other than strengthening the barriers that separate us; barriers between his ill-informed perspective and the reality of what people of color face each day in this country.

Another time, I participated with several of my cousins in leading a discussion following a screening of *Traces of the Trade*. After many people had already spoken, a middle-aged man stood and said, "My ancestors owned slaves." His voice was unsteady, unsure. He paused for a moment and looked around the large auditorium filled with three hundred people; black, brown, and white women and men. He said, "This is the first time in my life I have spoken those words out loud. Watching this presentation and listening to so many people speak so openly . . . I feel like, for the first time in my life, maybe it's okay to talk about this. I hope I have the courage after I leave here to talk with my family about it."

I've never forgotten that moment. That guy gives me hope. When more white people, especially men, muster the will to speak up—*with each other*—then they'll be exposed to these issues from people they know. And when we white people, again especially men, take the time to stifle our inclination to share our vast wisdom and brilliant viewpoints at every opportunity—when we simply shut up—and listen, we may just get to a better place.

Sharon's Story

It takes a long time and a lot of lessons to learn what it means to be black. There is much variety in skin color in the African American community. Families range from the lightest white to the darkest black. My mother and oldest uncle had white skin. My other uncle and aunt were tan. My father and one of his brothers were dark brown. As a kid, I lived in a world that was predominantly black. Like most small children, I was oblivious to the differences and implications. I just knew automatically who was like me and who wasn't. The "one-drop rule"—a historical colloquial term—defined individuals with *any* African ancestry as black. To this day black people may have conflicts about skin shade, but persist in using this rule to define who we are.

My sister and I talked about this one day as adults. Lisa, who has brown skin, said she always envied me because of my near-white complexion, which she thought of as the key to a better life. In a twist of irony, I admitted that I felt the same about her, viewing her skin as more beautiful and a key to self-validation.

Both of my grandmothers were white. I never consciously thought about what race they were; they were just my grandmothers. They were seamlessly adopted into the black community. One of them had no white friends. The other had only one, who was also married to a black man. As I grew older, I overheard many conversations about racial issues. Generally, they revolved around something bad caused by white people. I officially learned about races in a science class at Catholic school when we talked about biology and genes.

I will never know why my maternal grandmother chose to marry a black man in 1926. Jennie Waymoth came to Chicago from a small farming community in Sidell, Illinois. Her ancestors were Scots-Irish. Her great grandfather was one of the early settlers of Illinois, where he migrated in 1826 from Kentucky. The family never owned slaves, and they fought on the Union side in the Civil War. That didn't stop them from being prejudiced.

She and my grandfather, Louis Nicholson, met at the restaurant in the Illinois Central train station in Chicago. He worked on a train. She was a waitress. The family story says Jennie had likely never seen any black people when she was growing up. When she beheld Louis, she was fascinated with his brown skin. He was attracted to her pretty legs.

After they married, her family pleaded with her to come home, even after she had two children, both of whom looked white. When her third child, my uncle Irving, was born with skin color that matched my grandfather's, they disowned her.

In 1932, Jennie went to visit her sister Sylvia, who also lived in Chicago; she took her three young children with her. Growing up, Jennie and Sylvia were inseparable. Jennie was stunned when Sylvia looked at her brown-skinned son and snapped, "You better get away from my door. You know Walter doesn't want any niggers in his house."

Jennie never visited her sister again. She never went back home to Sidell to live. She stayed with her husband in Chicago, gave birth to a fourth child, also tan-colored, and came to be known and loved as "Maw Maw." When I spoke with a Waymoth descendant in the 2000s, I was told they thought Jennie had died. She was surprised when I informed her otherwise.

I could not fathom how my grandmother's family could disavow their flesh and blood simply because she married a black man. How could they feel so superior? But then, she sometimes did things that made me wonder which side *she* was on. Walking in public with my younger sister, a babe in arms, she covered up her brown-skinned face with a blanket. When she lived in California, she instructed my Aunt Janet to cover her less-than-straight hair with a scarf. My uncle had told us how she refused his visit in the hospital. Was she prejudiced or were these choices forced upon her by society?

I found her relatives online. We had many pleasant conversations as I shared the details of my grandmother's life. They were happy to know she hadn't died as they had been told. We agreed that I would visit them, but there was a catch.

When I called to plan my trip, I was informed, "My mother lives with me and still keeps the old ways. She would not want a black person sleeping in our house." I felt what my grandmother must have felt that day on her sister's porch, even though I had not planned to stay at their house in the first place. I have had no further contact.

My paternal grandmother was Antonia Dora Federicho. To me, she was "Mama Dora." She gave my mother $100 for naming me Sharon Antonia in her honor. I spent my summers in Rockford, Illinois, with her.

Dora's father arrived in America in 1878 from a village near Naples, Italy. Al Capone's mother and Dora's mother were girlhood friends in the tiny village of Castellammare di Stabia. The proudest moment of Dora's father's life was when he became a naturalized American citizen. The family moved to Chicago from New York before Dora turned four. Al Capone moved to Chicago in 1919. He set my grandfather up in the bootlegging business during Prohibition.

In 1922, Dora and Robert Leslie caught each other's eye at Ford's Laundry, where they both worked. Dora was twenty years old when they married later that year. Because of his light brown skin and straight hair, her family thought he was a "dark Dago." By the time they found out otherwise, it was too late.

Mama Dora was not fond of white people. As I read the history of Italians in America, it was easy to see why. Italians were never slaves, but they suffered extreme prejudice and violence at the hands of white Anglo Saxon Protestants. They were restricted to low-income, low-class jobs and attacked for their Catholicism by the Ku Klux Klan. In 1891, eleven Italians were lynched in New Orleans in one of the largest mass lynchings in American history. Five shopkeepers were lynched in 1899 for giving equal status to black customers in Tallulah, Louisiana. During World War II, Italians thought to be loyal to Italy were incarcerated in internment camps, just like the Japanese.[1]

Mama Dora said white people were evil. She built her life around us and avoided them. I never knew her to have a white friend.

Thanks to her, I became an independent, opinionated woman. She taught me to think for myself, rely on myself, and not take crap from anybody. She was the first woman I knew who carried a handgun—a twenty-two-caliber pistol, which she carried in her purse. When I grew up, I followed suit. I met other members of her Italian family for the first and only time at her funeral in 1983, when I was thirty-two years old.

By the time my grandmothers had both passed away, I was well and truly done with white people. Although I still had to work with them, I no longer cared to understand what it was that made them so brutal, immoral, and intransigent.

My mother shared many stories that seared this into my mind. One of them was about the time she lived in New Orleans. She got a job working for a white family as a child minder. When they found out she was black, her job duties changed. They gave her their dirty laundry to wash. She quit.

Back in Chicago, she got a job as an elevator operator at The Fair Department Store downtown. When her employer learned she was black, she was fired. Black people were encouraged to shop at the store, but operating the elevators was a white person's job.

I was twelve years old in 1963 when President John F. Kennedy was assassinated. Black people surmised it had much to do with his championing of civil rights. In the later 1960s, I embraced the work of Rev. King. After he was killed, riots erupted in the streets of Chicago. The mayor responded with a "shoot to kill" order. I found myself trapped in the student administration building at the University of Illinois. It didn't matter that I was attending college and trying to make something of my life. That order applied to me.

Tom's Story

I was born in 1954, the year the Supreme Court handed down its decision in the *Brown v. Board of Education* case that outlawed "separate but equal" schools.

In 1963, I sat at my desk in Mrs. Anderson's fourth grade classroom at San Jose Elementary when Mr. Monteith hurried across the grass lawn that separated his fifth-grade classroom from ours. His muffled shout through the closed windows stunned us. "The president has been shot!"

Since there was a television in his classroom and not ours, we walked single-file to join the older kids in watching the news. Walter Cronkite announced that President Kennedy was dead. I cried. Our teacher encouraged us to pray if we wanted to. Though the Supreme Court had banned public prayer in schools, she told us it was okay to pray silently to ourselves.

When I first heard the name Lee Harvey Oswald, I decided that an appropriate punishment would be for the police to bring him to everyone's house in America so that each of us could punch him in the stomach. I was home alone watching television two days later when he was murdered by Jack Ruby.

All I heard was that Oswald was a deranged, sick man. There was no talk of civil rights or Martin Luther King in connection with President Kennedy's assassination. A few years later, I learned about Dr. King in junior high school. Dick Wing became youth minister at our church at about the same time. He talked with us about King and the civil rights movement. Some of the "cooler" kids in our group introduced me to the music of Bob Dylan, Jimi Hendrix, Cream, and John Mayall. I read books by Eldridge Cleaver and Dick Gregory. As my awareness grew, so did my apprehension in the face of anger I saw expressed by black kids at school.

The day after Dr. King was assassinated, I overheard a white girl say, "My daddy said he wasn't surprised at all. He expected King to be killed."

Though I was only fourteen years old, I knew there was much wrong in the world. I marched into the Robert Kennedy for President campaign office in Pomona and offered to hand out pamphlets. My school briefcase sported a Bobby Kennedy for President bumper sticker. My dad woke me up early one morning in June 1968 to tell me that Kennedy had been murdered the night before at the Ambassador Hotel, just thirty miles from our house.

Racial unrest the following year resulted in police in full riot gear patrolling the halls of my school. That year—1968–1969—would be my last in public schools.

Sharon's Story

In high school, I found only a single paragraph about slavery in my history books. It painted the institution as benign. In my sophomore year, I had two history teachers, Mr. Lawson and Mr. Martin, who filled in the blanks of the "official" version. They were both committed to telling the truth about American history, using books that were not on the approved list. We learned about slavery, colonization, the Middle Passage, the Haitian revolution, pan-Africanism, Black Nationalism, and slave revolts. My radical reading list made it clear to me why slaves were not allowed to learn to read. I was horrified, sickened, and angry.

At my all-black, inner-city high school, few of us were encouraged to pursue higher education. Somehow I made it to college. Once I got there, I was at a total loss. I didn't know how to cope because I couldn't understand being forced to learn things that had absolutely no relevance to my life. I balked at the class in Finnish dancing and retreated to the social room, where I spent my days playing cards for money. I earned enough to pay for the few semesters I attended school. I dropped out to take a full-time job.

Shortly after leaving school, I had a desultory love affair and, in my ignorance, ended up pregnant. I was a stereotypical ghetto girl, destined for a life on welfare. When I went back to school in the 1970s, I was accused of cheating on the entrance exam at the city college. I scored 99 percent. I don't know if they ever believed I didn't cheat, but they let me in.

When Black Panther Party deputy chairman Fred Hampton was murdered in Chicago in 1969 by a barrage of bullets as he lay sleeping, I mentally prepared myself for revolution. He was killed by a tactical unit of the Cook County State's Attorney's Office, supported by the Chicago Police Department and the Federal Bureau of Investigation.

As the eighteen-year-old mother of a newborn son, I realized his chances were bleak. In six short years, John F. Kennedy, Martin Luther King Jr., Malcolm X, Robert F. Kennedy, and Fred Hampton had all been shot dead. I wasn't about to teach my son to turn the other cheek. I began attending meetings at the sandbagged headquarters of the Chicago Black Panther Party.

Tom's Story

Until I was twelve years old, almost everyone in my life was just like me. My world was a white one. All the kids in my neighborhood were white, except for one Cuban boy. Almost all the kids at San Jose Elementary were white. Almost everyone in our church and in my Boy Scout troop was white. In junior high school, for the first time, I interacted with significant numbers of people who were *not* white.

Then, in 1970, when I was sixteen years old, my family moved ten miles from Pomona to Glendora. My parents had already removed my sister and me from public school and enrolled us in Western Christian High School to escape racial unrest and the fear that one of us might be injured or that the atmosphere might traumatize us. Though I wasn't much of a singer, I joined the choir at my new school. I had an ulterior motive. A trip was in the works for the spring of my sophomore year. The choir would travel across the United States and back by bus for an entire month. We would share the Gospel of Jesus through song at churches and Christian colleges along the way. It was an adventure too enticing to pass up.

I had spent my entire life in Southern California; this was my first chance to travel to New York, Florida, and many other states. We would visit the Washington Monument, Times Square, Jamestown, and Williamsburg. Less than two hundred miles from Williamsburg, we would sing at a school I would later encounter under much different circumstances: Eastern Mennonite College in Harrisonburg, Virginia.

I don't remember much about most of the places we went. I recall riding for hours and hours with my friends and our chaperones on the bus. And I remember one particular church in Birmingham, Alabama.

When our bus pulled up to the curb, we piled out. Several of us were thirsty and looked around for a drinking fountain. Spying one nearby, we made a beeline for it. As I bent to drink, I heard the stern voice of the church's minister. "That fountain is not for you. Yours is over here."

That's when I noticed the sign that said, "Colored."

I'd heard of such things, but thought they were ancient history. I'd been sharing drinking fountains, classrooms, bathrooms, and showers with black kids in junior high, as well as at sporting and cultural events, for years. How on earth such a system was still enforced in 1970—and in a church, no less—was mind-boggling.

Through the magic of Facebook, I've reconnected with several high school classmates—most of whom I've had no contact with since 1972. Lavona "friended" me and we began to reminisce; writing back and forth about our lives and other classmates.

At one point I asked about the choir trip and if she remembered that church.

"Seeing that sign was a life-changing moment for me," she wrote. "It broke my heart. It had a profound effect on me for the rest of my life. I realized that there was more to life than our typical white exposure that we had been fed in school."

"What's so weird," I responded, "was that it was 1970. Civil rights legislation was signed in 1964. Segregation was outlawed. Yet the church still practiced it."

With Lavona's encouragement, I contacted other classmates.

"I definitely remember that church," wrote Peggy. "I don't remember the fountain incident. Some of us wanted to use bathrooms near the front of the church because they were closer to the choir platform. We were told those were for blacks. I felt like I was in the twilight zone. I just couldn't get it to register for quite a while." Peggy's comment came as a surprise. I didn't know about the bathrooms.

Phil also used the bathroom. "I walked in and remember thinking it was very run down. Then I was informed that it was for colored people. I later found the restroom for white people was much nicer."

I called Terri. She was horrified. "I clearly remember seeing the 'colored' sign. Afterward, we all gathered back on the bus. The choir director, Mr. May, tried to keep a lid on things. He reminded us that we are guests. We have a job to do. He was kind of freaked out."

"Yeah," I said, "I remember being told that people in the South have different beliefs and customs than we do; that it was important that we show respect and not question certain things."

"I was really sad," she said. "There was an underlying current of terror that I could feel. As we drove through the Deep South we passed row after row of old, ramshackle cabins with people sitting on the porches. I buried my head in my lap so I wouldn't have to see it anymore.

"I thought about all the history of this nation and all that white people have done wrong; the sense that 'we're better and they are less' was clearly at the core of beliefs. We watched the elderly, the poor, and knew their opportunities were less than ours. It was so different seeing this with my own eyes instead of just in books or magazines. And it was so hot and merciless.

"To this day when I visit the South I still expect to see people wearing white sheets. Witnessing such separation at that church—and this from Christian people who are supposed to love everyone—I felt so much evil and violence and knew that black people must be terrified."

Several of my classmates, including Larry, recalled us singing the *Battle Hymn of the Republic* in Birmingham that evening. Larry's family has Southern roots, and his family was concerned. Marv, our bus driver, requested aloud during the service that we sing it. I felt shocked and scared when I heard his voice. We weren't supposed to sing that song in the South; only in the North.

"It infuriated Mr. May," wrote Valerie. "He put Marv in his place. Mr. May could've refused. Yet, it was more than one hundred years after the Civil War. This is so much to think about, isn't it? I remember our teachers hovering over us more in the South than elsewhere on our journey."

Mr. May also remembers the incident. Lavona found our old choir director on Facebook and put the two of us in touch. When I spoke to him by phone, the first time I'd heard his voice since high school, the voice that once struck terror in me whenever I was in trouble, he chuckled at the memory of Marv requesting *The Battle Hymn*. "That was an awkward moment."

He told me that the church was a Christian and Missionary Alliance church, located next to a police station in Birmingham. Mr. May had been ordained in that denomination and knew the pastor. He remembers the "white" and "colored" facilities as well as the fact that there were a few, not many, black members of the church. "As awful as it was, it was the culture of the day. I do hope those days are behind us forever."

Sharon's Story

I was surprised when Tom told me this story. I had never considered such things from the opposite side; how white people felt about separate fountains and other separate things. After all, they were the ones who made them separate in the first place.

I never had such experiences growing up. There were no white and colored water fountains in Chicago. We could sit anywhere we wanted on a bus or train. My environment provided a cushion that shielded me from many hurtful things. The racism and segregation in the North was more subtly delivered. In spite of my lack of personal experience, the power of Jim Crow rules were impressed on me by my elders. They bore the brunt of so many indignities that, even today, I find it hard to comprehend. My genealogical treks through the South provide me with a window into their lives.

A friend once told me when, as a child, he saw his first "colored" drinking fountain, he *really* wanted to try it because he thought it would spout a rainbow of colored water.

As a kid, I remember not being able to use public bathrooms when we were on the road. We had to pee in the bushes along the road. I thought my stepfather just didn't want to stop. When my mother traveled cross-country by car with my uncle, they avoided restaurants along the way because of my sister's brown skin. In Texas, they were told to go to the back door to be served. That was 1963. She returned home furious.

THE GREEN BOOK

A travel guide was published in 1936 to help black people stay safe on the road. *The Negro Motorist Green Book* listed hotels, boardinghouses, restaurants, beauty shops, barber shops, and other businesses that served black people. The introduction read:

It has been our idea to give the Negro traveler information that will keep him from running into difficulties, embarrassments and to make his trips more enjoyable.

There will be a day sometime in the near future when this guide will not have to be published. That is when we as a race will have equal opportunities and privileges in the United States. It will be a great day for us to suspend this publication for then we can go wherever we please, and without embarrassment. But until that time comes we shall continue to publish this information for your convenience each year.

Publication of *The Negro Motorist Green Book* ceased after the passage of the Civil Rights Act in 1964.[2]

South *and* North, black and white governed *everything* about people's lives. As late as 1967, seventeen American states still had laws on their books against miscegenation. Many cities and counties, and some entire states outside of the South, had laws forbidding black people from taking up residence within their boundaries.

Sharon's Story

When I lived in Atlanta in the early 1970s, my most shocking experience was reading an ad in the *Atlanta Constitution* announcing a Ku Klux Klan rally. This wouldn't be the last time I encountered the KKK.

Two decades later, in 1994, I headed up a project in Mobile, Alabama. I was invited to dinner one evening soon after I arrived by a man who said he wanted to feed me before the town killed me—as I was doing something so radical I surely wouldn't live to see it through.

It started out as no big deal, at least as far as I was concerned. I organized a spring break event for African American college students. I did so at the behest of my son, who attended Howard University, a historically black college in Washington, DC. Vincent got the idea from another big spring break event called "Freaknik," which was held each year in Atlanta. Just like another annual congregation of white students in Florida (this one didn't have a name), Freaknik drew thousands of African American young people for a weekend of partying, gawking at each other, and tying up traffic. We designed an event that would feature cutting-edge musical artists, authors, community activists—a range of people with something productive to say. After evaluating several potential locations, we selected Mobile. The tourist agency for the city encouraged us. There were plenty of venues for the music, great places for parties and picnics, a white sand beach in nearby Gulf Shores, and locations of historical significance to black history. All the ingredients were present for a landmark event that would surely draw crowds.

The last ship to bring slaves into the United States from Africa provided our historical link. Although slave importation had been outlawed in 1808, the schooner *Clotilde* sailed into Mobile Bay in 1859 with more than one hundred people aboard. Federal authorities lay in wait. The captain transferred his cargo to riverboats and set fire to the ship. It sank. After Emancipation, the people brought from Africa on the *Clotilde* reunited and established a community known as "Africatown," which still exists. Our schedule included a program to commemorate this history.

We planned to call our event "Buck Wild in Bama." The name was a nod to sensationalism. If young people were enamored of "Freaknik," "Buck Wild" was the way to go. We were aware of the historical connotation of black men going wild, but wanted to convert it into something positive. I defended the name when called before the city council. It didn't work. We were forced to change the name to the much tamer "Breakout for Spring."

When I was interviewed on a radio program, it ignited the ire of the entire white community. They burned up the phone lines, wanting to know, "Why in the world do you want to make an event for *black* students?" It did not register that our students are just as entitled to a spring break as theirs.

While reviewing accommodations at the state park on the white sand beach of Gulf Shores, I was escorted into the police station and shown the cell I would be put in should any person attending my event do anything whatsoever to cause a problem.

The last straw was when I met the founding grand wizard of the Mobile chapter of the Ku Klux Klan. He owned the daily newspaper. This ninety-year-old white supremacist proudly proclaimed his credentials and questioned my right to bring an event to his state.

"I have roots in Alabama," I snapped, "family members buried in Montgomery, and just as much right as anybody else to be here."

I asked a white friend to fly in from California to infiltrate the opposition. He pretended to be an event sponsor and organized a meeting with members of the Mobile "powers that be." He returned after that meeting whiter than I had ever seen him. They told him things in the meeting he was too ashamed to repeat. He produced a plane ticket and urged me to leave immediately and go to California with him. When I refused, he left me there.

By then it was a matter of principle. I could not confirm one sponsor, and had spent all my own money, but I plodded ahead anyway. In reaction to my stubbornness, the "city" did everything they could to destroy the event. Threatening-looking white men followed us everywhere, making a point of being seen. The headquarters hotel told musical artists they had no rooms reserved for them. The weather service issued a bogus hurricane alert and advised people to stay away.

The police chief, who was African American, took me under his protection. Members of the Fruit of Islam, the security force for the Nation of Islam, arrived unannounced one day from Birmingham. Brother Terry, the leader of the contingent, said, "Sister, you are in deep trouble and we are here to watch over you."

In the end, the event failed miserably. Although police reports said at least five thousand students turned up, we couldn't operate past the first day. I had run out of money. Devastated financially and emotionally, I made sure everybody else got back home, then borrowed money to fly to California, where I enrolled in bartending school and worked as a secretarial temp. I earned enough money to buy a ticket to South Africa. It was my intention to never return to the United States.

CHAPTER EIGHT

Cycles of Violence

Violence is intrinsic to the American way of life. European immigrants largely annihilated the indigenous people they found here, "tamed" the rest by sending them west to reservations, and enslaved millions of African people. They confiscated lands in the Southwest by making war on Mexico, and in almost every generation engaged in major warfare. From Europe to the Far East and beyond, the United States has left its mark. It was the first and only country to attack another with nuclear weapons.

Americans are nurtured on stories of conquest and war. Is it any wonder that these collective experiences would inform the modern technology that has enabled people to become increasingly inured to violence and its effects? Slasher movies idealize psychological terror and extreme physical violence. Computer games aggrandize tactical weapons skills rooted in warfare.

The short list of race-related violence includes racial anthropology, freak shows, eugenics, forced sterilization, medical experimentation, miscegenation laws, terror campaigns, destruction of black towns, race riots, lynching, Jim Crow, voter disenfranchisement, land grabs. The past and its violence continue to live. They impact us in ways that we may not understand. The legacy has an effect not only on people who immigrated to America from other countries in the past, but those who immigrate today.

Slavery has existed in every society and every culture throughout history. As Milton Meltzer describes in *Slavery: A World History*, prior to European involvement in the slave trade, most people became slaves because two societies went to war and the victors enslaved the losers. In America, more perniciously than anywhere on earth, slavery evolved into something quite different from other types that existed before—in treatment, length of servitude, and how the enslaved were viewed by their owners. Europeans created a new paradigm. Traditional forms of domestic slavery and indentured servitude evolved into a competitive profit model. The system relied on an extreme form of racism with which Europeans convinced themselves that Africans, in Meltzer's words, "were 'naturally' indifferent to human life, and that they could not take care of themselves and needed the kind of care of the 'great white father.'"

It is important to recognize that every time a system of oppression to keep black and brown people down has reached its end, another has been implemented to take its place. After two and a half centuries, slavery became unacceptable in the United States. It took a horrific war, hundreds of thousands of casualties, and the resolve of many people, North and South, to end slavery. A dozen years of hope, known as Reconstruction, followed, during which emancipated black people exercised their right to vote and succeeded in getting elected to public office. White supremacists then promoted a new system to keep black people "in their place" at the bottom of the social and economic ladder. Jim Crow—the legally and socially sanctioned system of segregation, discrimination, and terror—ensued.

When the Jim Crow period ended, there was another brief moment of respite in the victories of the civil rights movement. Then, as Michelle Alexander outlines in her book *The New Jim Crow*, another evolution took place. President Richard Nixon implemented the "Southern Strategy," promulgating the idea that the way to maintain the power structure with white men at the top was to divide poor white and black people by convincing the whites they had it better. With hard work and a little luck, they could achieve the American Dream. If not, well, at least they weren't black.

Nixon used blatantly racist tactics to succeed politically. Incorporating vitriolic law-and-order language (blaming black people and communists for riots and unrest), he and others set the stage for a shift to a new system. Thus began a new era of mass incarceration of black people in the prison system that continues today. With the creation of the war on drugs, people of color were targeted by law enforcement. Alexander cites horrifying statistics: By 1991, fully one-quarter of young black men were under the control of the criminal justice system. By 2006, although "people of all races use and sell illegal drugs at remarkably similar rates," 1 in every 14 black men was behind bars (1 in 9 for those twenty- to thirty-five years old) compared with 1 in 106 white men.

Both major political parties supported these efforts. The onslaught continued under Reagan and reached its peak during the Clinton administration's implementation of "tough on crime" policies, which resulted in the largest increase of prison inmates in US history. The system is now so deeply embedded it will take activism on the scale of the civil rights movement to undo it. It is unlikely that will happen any time soon because once a political tool becomes institutionalized, it is no longer a tool. It's just the way things are—much like segregated drinking fountains once were. It becomes the American way of life.

While acknowledging its flaws, we hasten to affirm that the criminal justice system serves many important functions—even though applied imperfectly and discriminatorily. Ideally, it denounces wrongdoing, draws boundaries on acceptable behavior, and identifies those who do wrong. It is supposed to protect due process and human rights. However, criminal justice as practiced in the United States is also adversarial, like a boxing match. It does not serve the needs of victims well, nor does it effectively hold offenders truly accountable. Throughout history, it has done a consistently poor job of dispensing justice equitably. It does not work to strengthen communities.

We believe the criminal justice system in the United States, and any discussion about healing racism within that system and elsewhere, needs to be reframed using a *restorative justice* model, which represents a powerful way to address the weaknesses in our systems. Restorative justice seeks to create a dialogue, to reexamine our assumptions about justice. It is a peacebuilding approach, one that is about creating, mending, and maintaining healthy relationships. It rests at the core of the STAR program and Coming to the Table.

Traditional criminal justice asks three questions: What laws have been broken? Who did it? What do they deserve? Restorative justice asks additional questions: Who has been hurt? What are their needs? Who shares the obligation to meet these needs? The differences in these questions are significant. Beginning with the concept of "wrongdoing," restorative justice can elicit profoundly different effects on both approaches and outcomes when harm occurs. Slavery, racism throughout society, and racism within the criminal justice system, and other systems, are violations. Violations create obligations. The central obligation is to repair harm and relationships. As applied within Coming to the Table, the goal is to begin a healing process that takes into account the harms of the legacy of slavery. The process starts with understanding how this legacy has impacted us all. The biggest challenge is finding ways for white people to understand and acknowledge that. In that regard, restorative justice allows space for listening, sharing stories, and dialogue. Before harm can be repaired, we first must share stories about the heritage of slavery and racism. We can then identify contemporary needs and strategies for repair and healing.

Ideally, we would hope to reach a point where white people acknowledge the racism that exists in them and in the society in which we live, the privilege that results for white people, the harm that has resulted for everyone, and the need for healing. Healing is a very broad term, different for different people. It can't be prescribed.

Dr. Howard Zehr, professor of restorative justice at Eastern Mennonite University, presented these concepts at the first Coming to the Table gathering in 2006. He is known internationally as the "grandfather of restorative justice." According to Zehr (see his *Little Book of Restorative Justice*), the concept of justice has mainly to do with fairness and balance. It's about proposing consequences for what has been done; consequences that are often painful.

Zehr suggests that restorative justice can help reframe the discussion of historic slavery, racism, privilege, and present-day inequities. There are four places in which restorative justice applies to this conversation. It recognizes harm that's been done, the needs that have come out of that harm, where the applications are to repair that harm, and engagement with all of those with a stake in it—and who ought to be involved in the resolution.

These conversations rarely make a connection between slavery and privilege and between slavery and racism. For white people, denial is a big obstacle, as is guilt. Those who are made to feel guilty put up barriers or strike out, which only increases the predisposition to denial. Zehr also believes that shame is something we need to understand better. Western society is in denial about shame even though so many of our responses are shame-oriented. He opines that shame lies at the root of violence.

In Coming to the Table, we've learned how many black families did not pass down their stories of enslavement because of shame. It is the same with white families. The shame can be so great that, with no way to understand how to relieve it, the impacts never diminish. Where there aren't ways to remove shame, it can lead to bizarre and unhealthy behaviors.

In April 2011, we interviewed Dr. Zehr. When we asked what would be most useful toward ending racism and healing from the trauma and legacy of slavery, he responded, "We need to see that slavery is an important part of who we were then and how we are now. Guilt and shame get in the way. America's identity as 'do-gooders' and 'we're out to save the world' complicates things. One key is educating ourselves honestly. Our identity as a nation is tied up in our stories. Understanding our narratives about slavery would be an important factor in the healing process."

Sharon's Story

Talking about restorative justice brings to mind the Truth and Reconciliation Commission in South Africa. I was living there when the TRC hearings took place in 1995. It was a court-like proceeding based on restorative justice. Like millions of others, I was riveted to the television, watching the process unfold.

Day after day, I would see a black mother crying in anguish over a lost child. Her greatest need was to find the bones—to give her child's spirit a proper resting place. Then, in contrast, I would see a white police commander showing not one ounce of contrition. I vividly remember Eugene De Kock, who was popularly called "Prime Evil." He was responsible for countless instances of murder and torture. In 1996, he was sentenced to a jail term of 212 years. He remains incarcerated to this day.

One of the critiques of the TRC was that it allowed white people to wash their hands of their role in apartheid and say, "It wasn't me." The same thing happened in Nazi Germany. The system or someone else was responsible. A lot of people said, "I was just following orders." In America, we do the same thing when it comes to slavery: "It was my ancestors, not me" or "My ancestors had nothing to do with it." In saying these things, people give themselves a free pass to ignore the ongoing privileges and injustices that are embedded in our society.

If you don't have the awareness of what your ancestors did to create and protect those privileges, it is surely difficult to understand why black people are angry, why we are paranoid, and why some of us don't want to be around white people. Integration was problematic for me. I believe it destroyed the protective community we had that helped us survive and thrive in spite of all the injustices. In order to integrate, we had to give up a lot of our culture—become more like white people and exist as lonely islands in a big white sea. A one-way street was created that led out of my neighborhood. As housing opened up to black people in other areas, neighbors moved away; businesses closed. I think there could have been a better solution, one that enabled us to retain our communities and still participate on an equal footing in the general society.

Tom's Story

Though my experiences differ greatly from Sharon's, issues of race and violence have still had an impact on me, one way or another, throughout my life. There were frightening moments that I remember vividly, and completely banal moments that I have to concentrate to remember. I suspect I'm not unique in stating that my most powerful memories are from the times I felt threatened.

I wasn't afraid of all black kids growing up. We joked in class and played sports together in PE. I held my own in the high jump. I always lost in wrestling matches because I was small and not particularly strong. We sat in the bleachers together and rooted for our football and basketball teams. Unlike my other white friends, I liked to hang out at the Teen Post, which was one block from my house. I often stopped there after school. The only other white kid I ever saw there was the director's daughter.

We gathered to play ping-pong and billiards. Couches and chairs filled one large room where I guess someone thought we might do homework. Blaring in the background was Wolfman Jack's radio show from

Tijuana. He played cool songs by black groups I'd never heard of; songs they never played on KRLA. I got pretty good at ping-pong. Slip a nickel into the machine and out popped a bottle of Coca-Cola, long after it went up to a dime everywhere else. I felt cool hanging out at the Teen Post. I made more black friends, which I thought would make things safer for me at school. I almost always had a great time. Then one day I was sitting on the couch drinking a Coke when a big kid named William, the most fearsome black boy I ever knew, stood directly in front of me and spat out the words, "Get up."

I froze in terror. Sometime back, I had been in the bathroom at school where I saw William turn and pee on the leg of a small white boy named Keith. I hurried out quietly, trying not to draw attention to myself. The last thing I remember was William laughing while Keith just stood there and took it. I guess William knew I saw him, because he now loomed tall above me with his rock-hard muscles bulging from his too-small t-shirt. I didn't say anything. I just stared and tried to quickly figure a way out of this.

"You told on me and got me suspended from school. Now get up, honky!"

"No, it wasn't me." I pleaded. "It must've been that boy Keith."

"It wasn't no Keith. You callin' me a liar?"

"No. No, I'm not calling you a liar. I just . . ."

"What are you sayin' then?"

I will never forget the pounding of my heart and the realization that I had nowhere to run. One punch from William and I wouldn't wake up until next week. I began to tremble.

William laughed. Everyone laughed. I hadn't realized that several others formed a half-circle behind William. He slapped my shoulder. "I was just messin' with you," and walked away. After that, I went to the Teen Post less often. Most of the kids remained friendly with me, but after my encounter with William, I was too uncomfortable.

And yet . . .

I loved drama class. If I couldn't be John Wayne in real life, I could act like him in school productions. One year, we performed *Bye Bye Birdie*, the musical based on a fictional account of Elvis Presley's induction into the Army. My mom was the pianist, so we practiced all the musical numbers at our house. Mine was one of the small but featured roles—Randolph McAfee, whose big sister Kim is caught up in the hubbub surrounding Conrad Birdie's induction. She is the girl in his fan club who will receive one last kiss on *The Ed Sullivan Show* before he ships overseas. My biggest moment came when I sang "What's the Matter with Kids Today?"

My friend Sam, a black boy, was cast as Conrad Birdie (the Elvis Presley character). Another friend, Nancy, a white girl, was cast as Kim. The whole point of "the kiss" is that it gets interrupted by Kim's boyfriend, Hugo, who punches Conrad in the nose. In our production, I clearly recall our drama teacher, Mrs. Sloat, telling Sam and Nancy that if Peter (who plays Hugo) misses his cue and doesn't stop the kiss, Sam and Nancy will need to go through with it. They were fine with that. But I knew, as did everyone, I'm sure, that this was a big deal. A black boy kissing a white girl in a junior high school play in 1967 could be trouble.

It wasn't. The play went off as rehearsed.

My role models at school also included black people in positions of influence. I loved math and my teacher Mrs. Moham. I wasn't skilled in wood shop, but Mr. Primus was patient. The science teacher, Mr. Buggs, undoubtedly interrupted several suspect experiments to keep me from blowing up the lab, for which I am grateful.

One day, a group of us were having what they called a "rap session" back then. I mentioned being good friends with one of the black boys, someone with whom I had many significant conversations in the past. When I said that, he scowled and asked dismissively, "When have we ever talked seriously about anything?"

I was embarrassed and hurt by his denial. Even though I tried, even though I thought I had good friends who were black, even though I wanted to make a positive difference, I learned that I didn't and I couldn't.

My childhood can mostly be described as a mirror of the programs I liked to watch on television. My favorites were *Father Knows Best* and *Leave It to Beaver.* Though my mom didn't wear pearls while baking chocolate cakes, it was pretty much idyllic. We went to church on Sundays. We went camping in the summers at Grand Canyon, Yellowstone, or in the High Sierras. My dad and I went to Boy Scout meetings every Monday night and camped out with Troop 101 one weekend each month. No matter how scared I felt at school, my life was mostly calm. And, with the help of my parents and other adult mentors, I was mostly successful in almost everything I tried to do.

Sharon's Story

White people appear to live inside a cocoon of safety. My life was surrounded by violence. I attribute it to a society that makes people violent, angry, and predisposed to turn on one another.

My stepfather was born in McComb, Mississippi. He came to Chicago in the 1930s, after his father died. I know little about his background. Once he had wooed and married my mother when I was six years old, he changed from charming suitor into worst nightmare. He was a mean and vindictive man.

He was proud of his success in marrying "the whitest Negro woman I've ever seen," but in spite of his attraction to her skin color, he *really* hated white people. He never gave details, but I know the state of Mississippi led the nation in lynching and the Ku Klux Klan was very active in his hometown. During the civil rights movement, McComb was noted as the bombing capital of the world.

Leonard's diatribes were grisly. He described in graphic detail what he would do to any white person who attacked him. "I would run him over in my car, switch gears into reverse, and run over him again. Then I would get out of my car and beat the crap out of his lifeless body with a tire iron."

Something *really* bad had to have happened to make him so vicious in his desire for revenge. He was also prone to having nightmares. While napping on the sofa, he would moan, groan, and jerk about as if fighting. He would awaken with a start and complain that "the witch was riding" him. We never knew who that witch was.

There was an equally disturbing undercurrent of violence in my father. I was only two years old when my parents divorced, but in piecing together their story, I was shocked to learn how extensively he brutalized my mother. The divorce papers reference many instances verified by witnesses: "The defendant struck her with his closed fist and knocked her down . . . the defendant beat her about her body . . . he beat me and I was bruised in my face and on my body . . . he kicked me in the stomach. . . ." The fact that my father was, at one time, a Golden Gloves boxer made these testimonies worse. How could he turn his trained hands on a woman?

After graduating from high school in a time when many others did not, my father earned his living doing whatever was available—anything to make money. He was a bouncer, a bartender, a boxer, and even a policeman for a short time. During my teenage years, he would pick me up in his Yellow taxicab. As we rode around, he would tell me stories. One that he repeated often was about my mother; how he was pulled over more than once by policemen who demanded to know, "What are you doing with this white woman in your car?"

There was one story he never shared. My mother did. It was about her being gang raped and beaten almost to death because of her fair skin and long straight hair. Black men were the perpetrators. One was a well-known boxer. Her violation was incomprehensible and indefensible. Worst of all, as she expressed to me, there was no recourse in the community or the courts. My father made a deal with the perpetrators, accepting a bribe in exchange for not pressing charges. My mother's final analysis was that, no matter how she looked, she wasn't white, and that meant there would be no justice.

Even though the men in that particular case were neither arrested nor charged, it was common knowledge in the black community throughout my adolescence that a rite of passage for black men was a trip to the police station for a good beating. In 2010, Jon Burge, a white police commander on the South Side, was convicted for torturing black suspects. Over a twenty-year period he brutalized more than two hundred men within the walls of a police station in the black community.

I believe slavery has a great deal to do with violence that is endemic in the African American community. Dr. Joy DeGruy speaks a lot about it in *Post Traumatic Slave Syndrome*. She posits that "three hundred and eighty-five years of physical, psychological and spiritual torture have left their mark." When I was growing up, it was normal for parents to beat their children, husbands to beat their wives, people to brawl in public, and normal citizens to carry guns.

Though my household was comparatively peaceful to the world outside, my mother was a screamer. She would threaten to knock me into the middle of next week. Fortunately, the laws of physics made it impossible for her to make good on that promise. Instead, she would slap the crap out of me so fast I didn't know what hit me. These corrections were enough to keep me on the straight and narrow most of the time.

On the next level up, my mother and stepfather argued a lot—loudly. They argued so much, it interfered with my homework. I couldn't think for all the noise. I was terrified of the prospect of them killing one another, although they seldom came to blows. The one memorable time they did, my mother was the aggressor.

Well, that's not quite right. She told my stepfather she wanted a divorce. He agreed immediately but said if he went, my sister was going with him. That was his way of beating her. He did it all the time to both me and my mother. On that particular day, my mother fixated on his threat about taking my sister, got a funny look in her eyes and went berserk. She came at him like a raging bull and pinned him against a wall by his throat.

The fear I saw in his eyes was the same fear I had felt on another day when she threatened to beat me. I locked myself in the bathroom, desperately trying to figure out how to jump out the third floor window without getting hurt before she broke down the door.

Uncle Louie and I got along well. But he used to beat his kids all the time. He was so abusive with his oldest son, my mother tried to adopt him away. She said it was because his birth when my uncle was only nineteen trapped him in a marriage and three more children in rapid succession. The strain was too much. He only beat me once, when I got caught up in something one of his children did. Somebody spilled all of the clothes out of a laundry basket and didn't pick them up. He demanded that the guilty party admit to the transgression. He and my aunt took turns whipping our bare butts with a belt and an ironing cord until one of us owned up. It wasn't me. I'm not sure if the one who eventually cried guilty really was.

My father took his frustrations out on doors. He could hit a solid core wood door with his bare fist and splinter the wood, not his hand. Needless to say, I was terrified of ever drawing his ire and am sure he smelled my fear. Every time I saw him, he would announce, without provocation, "You're not too old to be whipped, young lady." I cowered. Then, one day, I decided I didn't want to hear it anymore. I drew up to full height, clenched my fists and dared him to stop talking about it and just hit me. He burst into laughter and backed down. But he never threatened me again.

In adulthood, there were more lessons to learn.

When my first husband got angry over something I said, he punched me in the face. My first reaction was total shock—not from the pain as much as the fact that it was happening . . . to me. I screamed, "Stop, you're hurting me!" He yelled, "Yeah, I know," and bore down harder. I escaped his blows and fled. When I came back, I told him if he ever did it again, he was guaranteed not to wake up the next morning.

In retrospect, it is clear his violence was in reaction to other things that were going on in his life. That doesn't make it right but it makes it understandable.

I can imagine all these situations repeated in different forms in previous times. In my mind's eye, I see a mother being stripped of her child and going berserk. I see her husband wanting to stomp over the slave master with a horse until his body is unrecognizable. I see beating some sense into children so they won't transgress white people's rules. I literally feel the anger well up inside me with no place to go. When you can't strike out at the person who is hurting you, you internalize the feelings and do violence to yourself and others closest to you.

Seeing these things has made me conscious of my own inclination toward violence and determined to step off that wheel. The disclaimer is, I would absolutely defend myself if directly confronted with violence from another adult. I continue to believe in corporal punishment for children, although I would never lay a hand on any child in a fit of anger. In spite of my propensities, I am a peace-loving person. I do not willfully aggress other people in words or deeds.

I must admit I slapped my nephew once—after he slapped me. My hand drew back instantaneously and acted on its own. I suppose that is a good example of how ingrained the lessons of life can be. Our brain automatically leads us to respond to aggression with equal opposing force. For a moment, it works. The problem is, it tends to escalate and get out of control. The point here is that violence, just like racism, is something we inherit. It may be a human inclination that makes us react violently, but it is socialization that encourages us to give rein to that impulse.

In 2011, a group of white teenagers in Jackson, Mississippi, set out purposefully to find and assault "a nigger." They ended up killing James Craig Anderson, a black man who happened to be standing near the off-ramp of the highway where the teens exited en route to their mission. They beat Anderson unmercifully and drove over him in their car as the bloodied man stumbled to find help. He died on the spot.[1]

Situations like this make me believe that some white people must be pathologically inclined to do what they do. I won't say *all*, but definitely enough to keep me justifiably afraid. In the aftermath of that violation, James Anderson's family made an astonishing request for the prosecutor not to seek the death penalty. His sister wrote a letter that said, "We . . . oppose the death penalty because it historically has been used in Mississippi and the South primarily against people of color for killing whites . . . Executing James's killers will not help to balance the scales. But sparing them may help to spark a dialogue that one day will lead to the elimination of capital punishment."[2]

I could not believe it when I read that statement in the newspaper. I don't know if I could find it in my heart to be so magnanimous.

Although I have searched for evidence for many years, I have no details about the lynching of my grandfather's uncle, Henry Nicholson. I heard the story from my uncles, both of whom had been told about it as children, as had my mother.

A national wave of lynching occurred between 1882 and 1951. According to *Lynch-Law*, a book written in 1905 by James Cutler, "Lynching is a criminal practice which is peculiar to the United States." A study by the Tuskegee Institute reported that 4,743 people were lynched in the United States; 3,446 black and 1,297 white. Mississippi led the nation, with a total of 581 occurring up to 1968.[3]

Lynching was a popular means of control and source of entertainment for white people. Men would take their families to enjoy "barbecues" and "picnics" where the main attraction was a person, usually black, being strung up from a tree. Beating, burning, and shooting were other popular modes of execution. Hideous acts of torture and sadism were not uncommon. Men and women were burned alive, dismembered, castrated, and disemboweled. There are cases of children and entire families being eradicated. Ears and fingers were often kept as souvenirs. Commemorative postcards were dispatched to distant family members to mark the occasion.

Few people were ever brought to trial for the crime of lynching. There are few coroner's records or death certificates. Victims were frequently unnamed. Bodies often disappeared. To prevent prosecution, newspapers, sheriffs, and witnesses generally attributed the crime to "persons unknown." If the rivers and lakes of the country were dredged, I have no doubt many bones would surface. The only printed reference I have ever found that *might* be related to my grandfather's story is "four unidentified black men lynched Kemper County, Mississippi, October 28, 1909." Kemper County is where the Nicholson brothers sharecropped. Was this my great-great-uncle Henry? If not, who *were* these men? Someone would surely like to know. As in South Africa, how can you ever find closure for grief until you find the bones?

Around this same time, another uncle from Mississippi, Owen Gavin, was also terrorized. He was driven off his land in Oklahoma. Owen was born four years before the Civil War ended. His father was a white man, Robert Lewis Gavin, whose story is told in chapter 6. Owen grew up farming and had the good fortune of being able to read and write. When his mother and siblings were driven out of Mississippi, Owen, living under the guise of being Native American, somehow obtained possession of some farmland in Oklahoma and moved his family there. When oil was discovered in the area, "Night Riders" perpetrated repeated attacks that ultimately caused the family to flee in terror and separate. One of his daughters was violated. Everyone in the family was forced to watch at gunpoint; a soul-wrenching humiliation for her father and brothers in particular.

Owen ended up destitute in Des Moines, Iowa. Several February 1912 news clippings from around the country report that he committed suicide "by blowing off his head with a shotgun" after receiving a notice from the overseer of the poor. The notice demanded that he "leave the county lest he become a charge on the county."

Can you imagine being run out of Mississippi, trying to find peace, and then being terrorized and evicted from Oklahoma and finally suffering the indignity of being ordered to leave your new community just because you're black and poor? That's three states in one lifetime; none of them by choice.

Tom wondered earlier about whether or not his namesake grand-father ever saw any black people. Owen died 136 miles from where Tom's grandfather committed suicide in Rolfe. Even today, less than 3 percent of the population in Iowa is African American. How ironic that Tom's ancestor and mine both committed suicide in the same state using the same weapon—a shotgun.

I didn't have to experience the same horrors as my ancestors did, but the accumulation of indignities informed my decision to leave America, which I did several times.

I lived in Jamaica from 1984 to 1989. One day, as I walked through the market looking to buy some tomatoes, out of the blue, somebody shouted, "Look at the American!" I turned and saw a man pointing in my direc-tion. I looked all around to see who he was pointing at. Finally, it dawned on me. He was pointing at *me*. I had never thought of myself as an Ameri-can and I didn't want to be identified as one in a public marketplace full of other black people, especially during a time when the US-led Inter-national Monetary Fund was in the midst of destroying the Jamaican economy with a "structural adjustment" program.

I left Jamaica in great sadness after a devastating hurricane wiped out everything I owned. Hurricane Gilbert was the worst hurricane on record at the time—a category 5 storm. Although I tried to hang on, I did not have the resources to start over again in Jamaica. Five months after the storm, I returned to the United States, where I knew I could get work immediately.

My next foray abroad was in 1994, when I migrated to Johannesburg, South Africa. I arrived in July, ninety days after Nelson Mandela was sworn in as president. The air was electric with joyous expectations for the new "Rainbow Nation." After forty-six years of apartheid—the oppres-sive system of legally enshrined race codes, modeled on America's "sepa-rate but equal" doctrines and those of Nazi Germany—the black majority population had achieved political parity. After twenty-eight years of in-carceration, Mandela was elected president of a reformulated nation.

Many things were familiar to me in South Africa. The country's his-tory of slavery, racism, and disenfranchisement of blacks mirrored that of America. It was easy to make friends and to engage meaningful conver-sations about race and the uplifting of the 40 million black citizens who had endured half a century of apartheid under the rule of 5 million whites. I knew many Afrikaners who were vociferously committed to mitigating change. However, it is one thing to *say* that something has changed. It is another for that change to truly become reality.

I found that out on the night of June 11, 1995. That was the night my son was beaten almost to death in an unprovoked attack by two white policemen. According to an article in the local paper, the *Star*, "The assault came after he [Morgan] and the television presenter [a friend] were almost knocked over by a car at high speed while crossing a Melville street. There was an exchange with the two occupants [of the car] and Morgan's friend was allegedly punched in the face by the driver. The occupants got out and the friend fled." The policemen, dressed in street clothes and driving an unmarked car, proceeded to beat Vincent to a pulp. They kicked him about the face with steel-toed boots until he was unconscious. Once the friend returned with help (a uniformed policeman), the suspects followed the ambulance that was called for Vincent and tried to intimidate him and his friend at the hospital. They warned them that, should they file a complaint, "We're going to come for you."[4]

When I saw my son's battered face, I gasped in horror and broke into tears. I have never, before nor since, seen anyone so brutally beaten. Vincent's head was blown up to double size. His eyes were swollen shut. His skin was black and blue. He had thirty-seven stitches in his face. He could barely speak. It is amazing that he didn't have a concussion or permanent injuries.

In spite of the policemen's threats, Vincent filed a complaint. It took two years for his case to come to justice. He left South Africa in disgust before it came to trial but returned to testify at the request of the government. We were assigned an advocate who worked with us throughout the entire proceeding. I sat in court seething with the desire for revenge. I decided that, if these two policemen were not convicted, I would take justice into my own hands. Fortunately, I did not have to fulfill that commitment.

The magistrate sanctioned the policemen for their testimony, saying that it was full of "outright lies and contradictions." One policeman defended his actions by saying that he was coming to the aide of Vincent's friend, "who is white, as he feared he was being assaulted by Mr. Morgan, who is black."[5]

We never made an issue of this being a racially motivated attack. It was so horrendous, something that should never happen to any human being. Many of our friends argued that pursuing this case was pointless. They were quick to point out that similar things happened to almost everyone we knew and that the possibility of justice was, at best, elusive.

Neither Vincent nor I would accept that. We had come too far, from a situation too similar, to be deterred. We had already had enough of American violence against people of color. South Africa was the land of our dreams, where a virtual revolution was in motion in terms of race relations. We stuck it out and were rewarded with vindication.

Once the officers were convicted, fined, and prohibited from serving on the police force, Vincent's statement to the media read: "I hope this will be a lesson to all South Africans, particularly black people who have in the past been systematically victimized by both the police and the courts. Brutality and racist attitudes are no longer acceptable. There is a process whereby justice can be obtained."

Ironically, soon after the verdict, but before his expulsion from the police force, one of the officers shot himself and three others in a freak accident in the police station. He died. I felt a sense of relief, serene in the remembrance of a popular black saying: "God don't like ugly."

PART THREE

Forks of the Road

" . . . men can only know and come to care for
one another by meeting face to face, arduously,
and by the willing loss of comfort."

WENDELL BERRY
The Hidden Wound

CHAPTER NINE

Grave Matters

Frightening streaks of lightning brighten the blackened, late afternoon sky. Earsplitting thunder rumbles in the distance. Rain and hail fall so hard that traffic has come to a halt fifty miles northeast of Louisville, Kentucky. We can't see to drive. Highway 71 is a deluged parking lot.

Tomorrow, we will learn this dazzling storm is part of the system that created a tornado that leveled Joplin, Missouri, and killed more than one hundred people 550 miles west of us. It is Sunday evening, May 22, 2011. This is the first day of an adventure that will keep us on the road for several weeks. We are twelve hours and 750 miles from our starting point in upstate New York. We breathe a huge sigh of relief when we reach our hotel in Louisville.

Travel became a large part of this healing journey. We've spent time in many locations around the United States and ventured as far as Tobago. We decided early on that the best way to combine the elements of the Coming to the Table approach was to visit places and people important to us and our nation's history. This foray is a grand road trip that will take us through twenty-one states and the District of Columbia. We will drive more than six thousand miles and stop in every location where there are relatives, ancestors, and memories to mine.

Sharon's Jeep is packed to the gills with clothes, food, tools, an axe and shovel—even a tent in case we have to camp out. We squeeze her Shih-Tzu, Nemo, into the back seat. He is an experienced road warrior, having traveled with Sharon many times before.

Tom's Story

I've spent a great deal of time over the past decades researching and writing about my paternal ancestors who hail from the North and Midwest. On this journey I want to learn more about my mother's side—the southerners. My grandfather, Thomas Edwin Pinckley, was born in Kentucky. A twenty-page booklet about the Pinckleys was written in 1941. *Whence We Came* relies largely on oral history. "Old John" Pinckley, my four-times-great-grandfather, was a cobbler. While living in west Tennessee, he had a contract "to make shoes for the negroes on a neighboring plantation." Each season he made shoes for as many as two hundred "field slaves" and "a large number of house negroes."

Tompkinsville, Kentucky, is a two-and-a-half-hour drive south of Louisville. Monroe County Courthouse holds many records related to Pinckleys. My great-grandfather owned a lot of land. Records only go back to the Civil War, since the courthouse in Tompkinsville, and twenty-one others throughout Kentucky, were burned during the war. Though I hoped to locate a birth certificate for my grandfather, we are told they are held at the state archives in Frankfurt.

Since I don't find what I'm looking for, I'm ready to leave. But Sharon isn't. She found several references to Pinckleys that were not on my list. She gets frustrated when I show little interest in looking at them: "I take note of *everything* I find because you never know how they may connect later."

"I'm pretty much interested in my line," I say.

"Fine." She slams the huge record book closed with a resounding bang. "I'm going to let Nemo out of the car for a walk." She turns and bolts outside. I stay put.

She returns twenty minutes later. "Since you don't want any of these records I found, are you finished?" She's exasperated.

"I need your help," I say, "not your judgment. I'm not as experienced as you. Let's check all the records. How many are there?"

"About half a dozen."

There turn out to be three times that many. I write down every one for future reference. I'm sure they are related to my grandfather. Though I don't appreciate Sharon snapping at me, I'm glad she's here to help. Having two people makes the work go much faster. The tension between us melts as we peruse the records she got so huffy about.

The big "find" of the day was the marriage record of my great-grandparents. Resting loose inside the binder is a note, handwritten in pencil more than a century ago. *"This is to certify that we John T and Billie Jones have no objections to our daughter Maudie and David J Pinckley uniting in matrimony this Jan. 26, 1898."* Maudie was only sixteen years old at the time.

These are the moments family researchers treasure. Goosebumps pop up as I hold the small, delicate piece of paper in my hand. I'm surprised and grateful that no one else took it as a souvenir, which anyone could have easily done over the past century. Someday another relative will run across it and experience the same thrill I have today.

After we find everything we think we can, we drive eight miles to the southwest along a narrow, tree-lined country road. Our destination is Gamaliel, a tiny town—population 426—just north of the Tennessee border. Several relatives are buried in the Church of Christ cemetery there. We drive under the wrought-iron arched entry. The "m" in "cemetery" hangs crooked.

We park the car and begin searching for the name "Pinckley" on headstones. Sharon has a "sense" when it comes to cemeteries that will be repeated several times on this trip. There are a lot more people buried in this large cemetery than currently live in Gamaliel. We don't know where my ancestors are buried, yet Sharon finds them within a few short minutes.

I stand before the graves of my great-great grandfather and his three wives. He outlived the first two; the third survived him by eight years. Resting nearby are other people I've not heard of but to whom I am clearly related. Having found some, but not all, of the ancestors I believe to be buried here, we return to the car and drive a few blocks to city hall. We intend to inquire whether there is a cemetery association and a plot map. This is when we discover just how much Gamaliel fits the description of "small town."

We park between city hall and a bank. The front door to city hall is open. I walk inside. The building is deserted. The corridor echoes my "Helloooooooooo." I walk back outside and cross the parking lot to the bank. Inside, I approach the gentleman behind the counter. He tells me the clerk who should be at city hall has probably gone for lunch. On his nametag I read the surname of someone who intermarried with my ancestors.

"Do you know if you have Pinckleys in your background?"

"Oh, yes," he replies. "We sure do."

"Nice to meet you, cousin," I smile. "My grandfather was born around here somewhere and I'm trying to find our ancestors at the cemetery. Do you know how we might find a registry?"

"Why sure, hold on." He picks up a phone book, finds the name he's looking for and dials. "Paul, do you have a list of who is buried at the cemetery?" He pauses for the answer and then says, "Is it okay if I send these folks over to your house?"

I feel like I've just stumbled on Garrison Keillor's mythical Lake Wobegon.

I walk back to the car and we drive two blocks to a brick house right next to the cemetery. As we pull into the driveway, we are met by a man who also turns out to be distantly related. Paul is sexton for the cemetery. He consults a typewritten list of internments and confirms my ancestors are all buried in the same general area. We return and locate all but Old John Pinckley. The cobbler died the year the cemetery was established, in 1830. If he's here, the headstone is illegible. It's one of the dead ends that every genealogist faces at one time or another.

Sharon's Story

I get really pissed off with anyone's nonchalance about genealogical research. Tom doesn't get how important this work is to me. I have spent a lifetime looking for my ancestral connections. These records are sacred to me. They are the only link I will ever have. But I have to take a white man with me to uncover a gravestone because I am afraid of being assaulted for desecrating a precious white grave. He drives into a little town and—Boom!—everybody is present and accounted for.

"Welcome to 1898, Mr. White Man, here's your handwritten note."
"Why, thank you! It's lovely here in 1898."

As I write these words, I think about the time a few days later when we were looking for marriage records for *my* people. They are found in separate "colored" ledgers. Even in records, we are segregated. (I do have to admit that separate records come in handy sometimes; I don't have to look through everybody to find who I want.)

Marriage for black people was illegal during slavery times. People also didn't get to keep the names their birth families gave them. Slave-traders purposefully intermingled people of varying cultural traditions so they couldn't plan rebellions as they traversed the Atlantic Ocean. When they arrived on these shores, names were bestowed on them that had nothing to do with people's history or culture. Besides breaking us up, the slave-owners decided African names were too hard to pronounce. What a slap in the face, when I think about the consonant-laden names I have had to wrap my mouth around in my lifetime. At death, we were dumped in the ground with little if any ceremony. The single thing that survived the centuries is oral history—and little of that—to direct us to whom we belong.

Every find in African American research is a precious miracle. On that day in Kentucky, I was seething at Tom for being so cavalier, so entitled, so dismissive.

Tom's Story

The afternoon is late when we drive the two hours from Gamaliel to Clarksville, Tennessee. We're headed for Lawson Mabry's house, where we will spend the night. He is one of Sharon's genealogy correspondents.

They met online. He sent her a treasure trove of historical documents recovered from his cousin's attic. Their common thread was Dr. John Marrast, the owner of the plantation where Sharon's Alabama ancestors came out of slavery.

When we arrive at the upscale community in which he lives, it is obvious Lawson has done pretty well for himself. We will sleep in a gorgeous coach house on a beautifully landscaped property with a large main house, an enclosed outdoor recreation room, and an intricately paved patio.

It is a pleasure to meet Lawson, his wife Beth, and their children. Knowing the purpose of our visit, he has arranged a dinner party that includes his mother and cousin Susan. Lawson and his mother Harriet keep us in stitches as we talk about the past.

Sharon's Story

When I met Lawson online, I was surprised when he volunteered to send me a package of documents that were astonishing. One of his ancestors kept meticulous details of the operations of his plantation, written in old-fashioned handwriting. It was the first time I truly comprehended why African Americans are dependent on descendants of the people who enslaved us to resurrect our genealogy. They hold the records.

Lawson and I easily established a relationship. Soon after meeting, he invited me to visit and stay the night in Clarksville. Drawn in by his sincerity, I accepted the invitation despite my usual reticence. Today, I would never think of going anywhere near Clarksville without stopping for a visit.

I am not sure Tom understood my insistence on including Clarksville in our itinerary. My motive was for him to meet this white man who had done so much for me. He had offered emotional solace to an angry black woman who needed answers.

Carrying on the tradition of storytelling for which southern people are so well regarded, Lawson and his mama regale us with the two-hundred-year history of the Mabry family in Tennessee. We hear about "DeLord" (not God but an actual person) and the great-aunt who had a direct line to God—Anna Marrast Mabry Barr, who carried a calling card imprinted with the 23rd psalm. She went to the White House to present it to then-president Nixon. Upon being intercepted by John Haldeman—of Watergate fame—she informed him that her business was between God, Nixon, and herself and refused further conversation by leaving. She died three weeks later. You can't help but imagine if the course of history might have changed had Nixon entertained Anna's visit.

Tom's Story

The weather remains intense. Around six, as we sit together in the gazebo in Lawson's backyard, an earsplitting siren interrupts our conversation. It

is followed by a loud, garbled voice. We assume it is telling people to pre-
pare for potential danger, but is unintelligible. Lightning and thunder are
in full effect. Buckets of rain pour from the sky, buffeted by strong winds.
Sharon wants to go into the house. She is afraid.

We move to the kitchen and turn on the television. The Weather
Channel displays the projected path of a tornado. Lawson calmly informs
us that it will pass ten miles to the north, then turns and begins to dish up
plates for dinner. He's not worried one bit.

Lawson was right. Within an hour, the storm passes. All is well. Then
the frogs start up, filling the night with a cacophony of croaking that will
no doubt lull us to sleep when we retire to the coach house.

I waited until we left the Mabry home the following morning and were
driving toward Atlanta to bring up a subject I have been wondering about:
guns. I have been a hunter. My first wife's brother and father taught me
how to shoot, kill, and dress deer. I gave it up long ago when I was shot at
by another hunter. Listening to bullets whiz above my head as I huddled
next to a large rock was the convincer.

Sharon is a member of the National Rifle Association. She owns guns
and carries one with her on road trips. Some months back, we discussed
the matter. I was visiting her home, and she warned me to be careful walking around in the night as she keeps a shotgun by her bed.

"Are you serious?" I asked.

"Of course I'm serious. I live alone. This place is pretty remote. I feel
safer knowing I can protect myself."

That's when she told me, "I generally carry one on the road with me as
well. I've spent time in places with scary people around. I have been told
point-blank to be *very* careful wandering about the South on my own."

"Where do you keep it?" I asked.

"Right behind the seat."

"Where do you keep the bullets?"

She turned to me with an "Are you kidding me?" look on her face.

I let Sharon know I was quite uncomfortable with the thought of a
loaded gun in the car behind our seats. She laughed and said she'd think
about it. I didn't raise the subject again until now.

"Did you bring your gun?" I ask.

"Out of deference to you," Sharon replies without looking at me, "no."

"Is that the only reason or does having two of us help?

"It's not the only reason," she says, "but having two of us—one of them white—*does* make a difference."

I am curious about what difference it makes but hold my thought and ask instead, "Have you ever pulled it out?"

"On someone?" She glances at me. "No, but when I sleep in a rest stop, I keep it out of its carrying case, right next to me, with the safety on."

Sharon's Story

During this conversation, I think about white men in pickup trucks with gun racks. It used to be a common sight all over the South.

Gun sales skyrocketed after Barack Obama was elected president. I am not sure whether people thought Obama would promote gun control or if it was something else. I do know that black people have always been discouraged from owning guns. There was a pervasive belief that we would use them to aggress against white people. As it stands, we are using them to kill each other. Of course, this does not apply to me. I want protection in the event I am confronted with danger; a lone female on the road in unfamiliar territory around people I do not know or trust.

Tom being with me makes a difference. I believe, should we be stopped by another white person, especially a policeman, and more especially in a rural area where I am an unknown person of color, I am less likely to be endangered.

Tom's Story

Outside Chattanooga, Tennessee, before we cross into Georgia, the landscape is lush, green, forested, and wide open. Sharon says, "You see places like this and wonder why people say there's a problem with population explosion."

"There's sure a lot of open space," I concur.

"We've always thought white people made that stuff up to keep us from reproducing and living here."

I'm driving at this point and glance over to see if she's serious. She is. "They didn't want us being born at all."

I'm not sure where this came from or what to say. "Okay . . ."

"There's a foundation for this. During slavery, black women were encouraged to have babies to make more slaves. White men stepped up to the plate to 'help' them produce more abundantly. They fathered children and didn't skip a beat in either keeping them enslaved or selling them off when their wives complained. Look at Thomas Jefferson. Thereafter, well into the 1960s, black women were sterilized without their knowledge or consent. White people wanted them to stop reproducing."

She asks if I know about eugenics. I don't.

"Well," she says, "it was a big deal. Just like in Nazi Germany, many people and organizations wanted to control the reproduction of 'inferior' bloodlines. In Germany, that meant Jews, Gypsies, black people, and homosexuals. In America, it was code for only one group—black people. I thought it might have happened to me when I failed to conceive any more children after my son was born in 1969."

Sharon's Story

Margaret Sanger, the founder of the Planned Parenthood organization, was well known for her belief in eugenics. She promoted a "Negro Project" with the aim of restricting reproduction by black people. Her sage, Thomas Malthus, a minister, was one of the first people to popularize the idea that there was a population "time bomb." As researcher Tanya L. Green notes in a 2001 Concerned Women for America article, "The Negro Project": "Eugenicists strongly espoused racial supremacy and purity, particularly of the Aryan race. They hoped to purify the bloodlines and improve the race by encouraging the 'fit' to reproduce and the 'unfit' to restrict their reproduction. They sought to contain the 'inferior' races through segregation, sterilization, birth control and abortion."

I drop another bombshell. "Did you know the 'father of gynecology,' Dr. J. Marion Sims, practiced on black women?"

"No. I've never even heard his name before."

Sims conducted medical experiments on black women; excruciating vaginal surgeries without anesthesia. He was much more compassionate with white patients, believing they "could not tolerate surgery without ether."[1]

Tom's Story

I continue to be amazed at the magnitude of horror black people have experienced. I suspect the vast majority of white people are like me. We haven't been exposed to such information. That's part of our journey—learning things we didn't know about each other's worlds. It's sobering but I'm grateful for the education.

When we arrive in Atlanta, we drive directly to the King Center on Auburn Avenue; the final resting place of Rev. King and his wife, Coretta Scott King. We walk the short distance to his birth home, historic Ebenezer Baptist Church, and the visitor's center across the street. This is our first exposure to the many interpretive centers operated by the National Park Service that we will visit.

We meet with a friend of ours, Vanessa Jackson, who lives in Atlanta. She led part of a workshop we attended in Jackson, Mississippi, in January 2010, which focused on the importance of storytelling to relationship building and healing. We discuss some of the challenges we face, like getting stuck trying to figure out what to do with the rage people express. Vanessa says, "It's the hurt, the shame, the pain, and the loss. If we can't figure out tools for that, we can't heal."

We acknowledge that people can and do move on from the damage. When they manage to do so, they do really well. But doing well on the surface often masks brokenness inside. "This is a conversation about pain and oppression," Vanessa adds, "class as well as race. It's an ever-widening story, which is why it's hard to get a handle on. It's important to connect the past with present-day circumstances. The descendants of enslaved people are still suffering now.

"When you believe that life and people are valued, I don't care what century you live in; you just don't do horrible things to people. You cannot separate them from your own humanity if you have a belief about connectedness. Without being naïve, how do we get back to oneness? How do we have larger conversations about the jacked-up things we've done to each other? Then we'll find out how my story slams up against yours."

After our conversation with Vanessa, we drive another two and a half hours to Montgomery and check into our rooms at the Red Roof Inn. The following morning, we head out to locate a small cemetery near Braggs, Alabama.

Sharon's Story

I searched for many years for proof of paternity for my great-grandfather. I believe the man who fathered him was James E. Leslie. During slavery times, James was the local blacksmith. He operated a shop in the county seat of Hayneville. I visualize him making rounds to perform farrier duties at neighboring plantations—the Marrasts, the Reeveses, and other names familiar from my research. My goal today is to turn over a gravestone I found a couple of years ago.

The cemetery in which I believe James Leslie is buried is the well-kept New Bethel, owned by the Baptist church he attended. The first time I went there with a friend, I found the entire Leslie family in a grouped plot. The only one missing was James. As we stood over a toppled gravestone next to his wife, we discussed unearthing it. I was ready to dig in. My friend Boo tilted his head in the direction of a white man sitting on a tractor in a field a few hundred yards away. He was not plowing. He was staring at us.

Boo leaned in to me and whispered, "Oh no. I am not going to help you do this." He was adamant. "I'm not going to get attacked or arrested for desecrating some white man's grave just because of a hunch you have. These people might kill us."

Disappointed, I determined I would just have to come back for the big reveal.

Tom's Story

Today will be different. Sharon tells me that having a white man with her completely changes the dynamic.

"Nobody will give a second thought to seeing a white man visiting the cemetery filled with white people in this very white, rural community."

"We should take some flowers or something to place on the grave," I say.

When we stop at a roadside rest to check our directions, we find an abandoned red, white, and blue plastic beaded necklace adorned with several American flags. Since Memorial Day is just a few days from now, it seems perfect.

Finding the cemetery proves challenging. Though Sharon was here a couple of years ago, the location we find online does not match the roads we drive around on today. For the third time, we pass the same abandoned Spur gas station with the caved-in roof and tall weeds. We need help. We haven't seen a single person outside of a few pickup trucks speeding down this narrow, two-lane road. We pull up to a farmhouse with a pickup truck parked in the driveway, a gun rack in the back window.

I walk alone to the front door and ring the bell. I hear footsteps approaching and then the voice of a young boy. "Momma, there's some man at the door!" I can feel him squinting at me through the door viewer.

I say loudly, but gently, "I'm not from around here. I'm turned around and just need some help with directions."

"Momma!"

Several minutes later, I hear the click of the deadbolt being unlocked. A young woman with dripping wet hair opens the door. Her son peers from behind her. I explain that I'm looking for the cemetery. She smiles, gives me directions, and wishes me well.

A few minutes later, we pull up to the New Bethel Cemetery. Sharon recognizes it immediately. We get out of the car and look around. There are no signs of life in any direction. Sharon points out the field from which the man had watched her on her last visit. We enter through the gate at the far end of the cemetery, passing over the roots and under the wide canopy of a large, old oak tree draped with Spanish moss. We walk to the far end of the cemetery and easily find the Leslie plot.

Sharon, prepared with a small shovel and crowbar, gently probes around the edges of a face-down headstone. After the years she's waited to see if her hunch is true, it takes surprisingly little effort to dislodge it. I help her turn it over so as not to damage the old stone. Just below the prominent Freemason logo, it reads "James E. Leslie," the dates of his birth and death and the words, "He left a wife and three children."

"Three *white* children," Sharon snaps. "They'd never mention a black child."

"No," I said, "I guess not."

We replace the headstone—face up—in the spot from which we dislodged it. Any future visitors will not have to go to the trouble Sharon has. We take pictures. Sharon writes down everything engraved on the stone. We lay the plastic beads on the ground.

The question I don't ask today is one I've wondered about since Sharon first mentioned James Leslie. She always refers to him as the father of her great-grandfather rather than as her great-great-grandfather. It seems like she really doesn't want to acknowledge her white ancestry. It feels like there's a lot going on there.

Sharon's Story

I don't actively claim my white ancestry because my white ancestors did not claim me. I am not interested in being related to people whom I feel could be so morally bereft. All I have is DNA that proves my paternal great grandfather had a preponderance of Scottish blood. The rest is an educated guess gleaned from years of research that puts this man in the right place at the right time under the right conditions. James Leslie, or somebody like him, made a child with an enslaved woman and then totally absconded with the truth.

In the Gavin and Leslie families, the men were Confederates in the Civil War. Robert Gavin made two babies with an enslaved woman at the same time he was fighting to keep slavery in effect. Once she was free, he made fourteen more and couldn't marry her—it is doubtful he wanted to anyway, even if it had been allowed. That sounds pretty schizophrenic to me.

One of my grandmothers was disowned for marrying and making babies with a black man. The other one, though white, didn't like white people. What is my inheritance from that?

Tom's intuition is spot-on. White is not something I ever wanted to acknowledge or be.

HISTORIC PLACES AND SOCIAL GRACES

From the cemetery, we drive twenty-five miles on to Selma. Downtown, banners proclaim "historic places and social graces."

After a delicious lunch at the Downtowner restaurant—fried catfish, greens, black-eyed peas, macaroni and cheese, washed down with sweet tea—we drive across the Edmund Pettus Bridge. We see a group of students—they look to be in their early teens—walking across with their teachers, no doubt reconstructing the march that changed America nearly half a century ago.

We pull into a parking lot at the south end of the bridge and enter the National Voting Rights Museum. The museum pays homage to the courage and strength of those who "suffered hatred, bigotry, violence and sometimes death in order to gain the right to vote for African Americans in America." In 1965, the population of Lowndes County was 81 percent black, but not one was registered to vote.

Once inside, we join a group of middle school students on a tour. The docent has a distinctive voice that commands attention: deep and expressive. We listen with rapt attention as he tells the students about Jimmy Lee Jackson, who tried to stop a policeman from beating his eighty-two-year-old grandfather in 1965 during a voting rights demonstration. When his mother intervened, the cop raised his club to strike her. Jimmie Lee grabbed the officer's arm. The policeman shot him at point blank range. The nearest hospital that would accept black patients was thirty miles away. By the time they got him there, the damage was done. He died eight days later.

Selma's black community mobilized around this event and called on civil rights leaders to lead a march across the Edmund Pettus Bridge from Selma to the capitol building in Montgomery to demand the right to vote. A few days later, six hundred people gathered to march. On that first morning, the county sheriff ordered all white males in the entire county over the age of twenty-one to present themselves at the courthouse to be deputized. When the marchers walked over the bridge, they were greeted on the other side by a wall of state troopers, who beat the peaceful marchers unmercifully.

It took three attempts for the marchers to finally reach Montgomery. Eight thousand people set off across the bridge. It took five days to walk fifty miles. At night, they camped at farms along the highway owned by black farmers.

In spite of the presenter's voice and inspired delivery, the students appear bored. The guide then explains he was only eleven years old when the march took place and was arrested twice for his involvement in the protests.

"They threw us in jail and the only water they provided was in a trough. Since we were acting like animals, they told us, we could drink like animals."

The students' attention perks up. One boy wants to know, "Were you scared?"

"No," says the presenter. "I was with my friends. There were older kids in the cell who took care of the younger ones."

Tom's Story

After leaving the museum, we drive along the same highway on which the protesters marched toward Montgomery. Sharon asks, "What would you do if you were black and this was happening to you?"

"I don't know. I believe the support of everyone in the black community was important. You knew you weren't alone."

Sharon doesn't respond.

We pass the first campground where the marchers spent the night.

"What would you do if you had lived here then?" I ask.

Without hesitation, she says, "I would kill them."

I look at her. She isn't smiling.

"One settler, one bullet," she says.

"What do you mean?"

"It's a phrase from South Africa. If you killed one settler, even if it meant sacrificing yourself, that was one less white person to worry about attacking you, your friends, or family."

I don't know what to say. I remain silent. Sharon vents.

"At some of these places, I get so totally pissed off. It's unfathomable. It took a judge ten days to rule that peaceful protesters shouldn't be attacked by police?!! Eighty-year-old people being beaten? A man killed for protecting his grandfather? And, after all that, I am amazed at how apathetic black people can be about voting. What the hell is *that?!*"

Sharon stares straight ahead as she drives down the highway. Her hands grip the steering wheel with force. A tear rolls down her cheek. We ride in silence until arriving twenty minutes later at the Lowndes County Interpretive Center. After Sharon parks the car, we pause before getting out.

I say, "Thank you for sharing what you're feeling."

Sharon takes another deep breath and says, "Okay, I'm better now. Let's go in here so I can get pissed off again."

Sharon's Story

The Lowndes County Interpretive Center is located on the site of a former tent city. Black tenant farmers who participated in voting rights activities were evicted by their white landlords. They banded together and built temporary encampments, where they lived for almost two years as the voting rights struggle continued. The brutality of white people contrasted sharply with the resilience and courage of black people seeking rights that were supposed to be guaranteed by the US Constitution. Evidence of this struggle is all over the center.

This was a place I was adamant about visiting. My father's family came out of slavery in Lowndes County. It is very personal to me. As I anticipated, my emotions are raw and at the surface.

Back in the car for our return to Montgomery, I say, "It definitely gives me insight into how my ancestors would walk out of slavery and get as far as possible from this place and how my grandfather and father would never come back." I pause and stare straight ahead through the windshield. "I have to stop talking about it."

"Do you want me to drive?" Tom asks.

"No," I reply, "driving will help. It gives me something to concentrate on."

We drive in silence. The hot Alabama air blows through the open windows as we speed along Highway 80 thinking about how long and difficult the struggle was for the democracy touted in 1776 to be made available to everyone.

After an already emotionally exhausting day, we arrive in Montgomery in the late afternoon. We park downtown across the street from the Rosa Parks Museum at Troy University. This is the site where Mrs. Parks entered the portals of history by refusing to give up her seat on a city bus in 1955. Her action led to a yearlong boycott of public transportation in Montgomery. The museum offers interpretation, lectures, seminars, storytelling, and other programs. Artifacts include original historical documents and a replica of the bus Mrs. Parks rode that day. We meet Georgette Norman, the museum's director, who gives us a personal tour.

The children's wing includes history timelines and interactive computer stations that enable students to understand the boycott, what led up to it, and the people who were involved. Norman describes the Rosa Parks Museum as experiential.

"We don't try to rewrite history," she says. "We let people experience it as they would have experienced it at that time. They make up their own mind. Often, when considering past events, people tend to talk about them with present-day perspectives. People act out of that consciousness.

"For instance, schoolchildren come here, and we take them to the events of 1955. White children say they never would have been part of the gang mentality of that time. Of course they would. They do what the culture of the gang says. People don't pay enough attention to how influential the culture is in which we live. We go along with the culture."

She escorts us to the "Cleveland Avenue Time Machine" in the children's wing. On this oversized bus, a simulated robot bus driver navigates a high-tech ride through time. Room-sized video screens, sound, and other special effects transport us to a street scene from the beginnings of the Jim Crow era. We visit Dred Scott, Harriett Tubman, Homer Plessy, and other significant figures from long ago. What we see makes it obvious: things don't just happen in history, people *make* things happen.

CHAPTER TEN

The Crossroads of Liberty and Commerce

At every courthouse we visit in Mississippi, there is a prominent monument to the Civil War; a Confederate soldier standing guard on the lawn. At Forrest County in Hattiesburg, a sign posted in the front door announces the building will close on May 30 in celebration of Memorial Day and Jefferson Davis's birthday. Hanging on the wall inside is a tribute to Nathan Bedford Forrest, for whom the county is named. He was a founding member of the Ku Klux Klan. In 2011, the Mississippi state government proposed to issue a license plate in his honor.

A day of research at several courthouses yields fruit when Sharon finds many pages of records listing slave names. We depart the Amite County courthouse, our last for the day, and head for Natchez. We take the back roads to get a feel for our environment.

Along the way, we encounter a sign that stops us cold. We pull over, turn around, and retrace the past few hundred yards. It feels like we are a thousand miles from nowhere. There are no towns, homes, or signs of civilization, just a deserted intersection. It is the intersection of Liberty Road and Enterprise Road. We sit. We stare. Both street signs are weathered and old. The stop sign next to them is riddled with bullet holes. We ponder how often enterprise has taken precedence over liberty.

THE MIGHTY MISSISSIPPI

As a result of an unusually wet winter and spring, the Mississippi River and its tributaries have dramatically exceeded flood levels. Recent storms exacerbate the problem. A few days ago, we contacted the owner of the bed and breakfast where we have reservations. She assured us that even though the river is at historically high levels and certain areas of Natchez are indeed under water, her home is well above the elevation subjected to floods.

Linden B&B does not accept pets, so we leave Nemo with the local veterinarian. We then locate the more than two-century-old antebellum home where we will sleep. It is less than a mile from the vet's office. We turn into a long driveway canopied with giant oak trees. They drip with Spanish moss, which gives the place an eerie feeling until we emerge into full view of seven acres of finely manicured lawns.

Our host, Mrs. Jeanette Feltus, greets us warmly. She is a lively octogenarian; impeccably coiffed and fashionably dressed. The widow of the fifth-generation descendant of the woman who purchased Linden, her voice charms with a musical Southern lilt. We are her only guests this evening. We have her full attention.

Mrs. Feltus shows us to our rooms. Located upstairs, separate from the main house, they are furnished with antique tables, chairs, lamps, and four-poster canopied beds. Fortunately, there are no chamber pots. We enjoy the modern conveniences of both private toilets and air-conditioning. The wide porch outside our rooms is appointed with dozens of plants and comfy wicker chairs. In Tom's bathroom hangs a painting of African people picking cotton. They pull long cotton sacks behind them. The Mississippi flows serenely in the background, replete with a riverboat dubbed *Natchez*.

We drop our bags and drive downtown to a park perched high on a bluff. We gaze over the fence at the swollen river, where treetops are visible a dozen yards from the water's edge, their trunks submerged. Buildings are flooded and abandoned; shops are buttressed with protective sandbag barriers. A metal bench appears to float on water hundreds of feet from the opposite shore. The damage is so extensive, we are thankful the devastation did not impede our travel.

We proceed down steep, narrow Silver Street to historic Natchez

Under-the-Hill, where we enjoy a cool drink to relieve the sweltering heat. Afterward, we drive back up the hill for a fine Southern dinner—accompanied by live music—at Biscuits & Blues. The downtown area looks like a picture postcard.

Tom's Story

Staying at an antebellum home and touring a plantation in the Deep South were both Sharon's ideas. Totally. I wanted nothing to do with it. Lindi and I visited Charleston, South Carolina, and Savannah, Georgia, a couple years ago. As we drove by the entrance to a plantation that advertised "beautiful gardens" and "tours through history," my stomach began to churn. The image of terrorized black people overwhelmed all other thoughts. I had no interest whatsoever in treading on those fields of blood whose present-day owners, I was certain, wanted me to believe some still-longed-for *Gone with the Wind* fairy tales.

Little did I know that the grand entrance to the home Sharon found for us to stay in Natchez actually *was* the model for the plantation "Tara" in the 1939 film. The cover of the Percy Faith album "Tara's Theme from Gone with the Wind" is not an image from the film, but a photo of the front of Linden House.

Sharon's Story

Against Tom's wishes, I *wanted* to stay in an antebellum home and was determined to do so. If we were going to explore slavery, we couldn't do it without seeing both sides. Tom tends to recoil from unpleasant things. He can sometimes be so sympathetic with my story, but doesn't want to look at his own—not with the candor that I would hope. What made Linden House in Natchez different from Linden Place in Bristol? Not much. I know what life was like in the slave cabins and fields. What I want to know is what the hell was going on in the heads of the white people who lived in the mansions—how they could look out over their fields with those black people in the picture in Tom's bathroom pulling cotton sacks and feel okay with themselves.

The website that drew me to Linden House included stories of ghosts lurking there. A man wearing a top hat has been seen in the bedrooms in which we slept. There is a woman who plummets off the edge of the roof and disappears before she hits ground. I don't know who these people are but I'm glad they didn't appear while we were around!

I thoroughly enjoy the house and our hostess. My general sense of angst has been greatly dissipated. My relief has much to do with confronting an icon of history—going to the scene of the crime and emerging unscathed. It is easy to intellectualize the past because we will never experience it firsthand. Here was the best I would ever come to "firsthand."

To say that the wealth and luxury of the planter's life juxtaposed against the poverty and deprivation of the slave's was obscene is an understatement. I am relieved by Mrs. Feltus's effort to do justice of a sort to her family history. She tells both sides with sensitivity and only a smidgen of obfuscation.

Tom's Story

After a restful night, Sharon and I rise in anticipation of the genuine Southern breakfast promised by Mrs. Feltus. She shows us into the formal dining room. Like every other room, it is filled with antiques. The walls are adorned with John James Audubon and Alexander Wilson prints from the early nineteenth century. A coin silver dining set rests on the buffet. A "punkah" hangs from the ceiling. Invented in East India prior to electric fans, a servant pulled a rope to wave the punkah back and forth, which shooed flies and created a cool breeze. The person fanning would no doubt have been enslaved.

Mrs. Feltus directs me to the chair at the head of the table. I pause and look at Sharon. "Oh, no," she laughs. "This seat is mine." She's been clear all along that a key aspect of coming here is that she wants to experience what it was like to sleep in "Miss Ann's bed" and be served at "Miss Ann's dining table." I'm happy to defer.

We're surprised when Mrs. Feltus serves us herself. We barely see the African American woman in the kitchen who prepared our scrumptious eggs, grits, bacon, homemade biscuits, peach compote, orange juice, tea, and coffee.

SOUTHERN TRADITION

When we finish eating, it is time for a tour. Linden is a magnificent structure. Built around 1790, its grounds originally comprised one hundred fifty pastoral acres. As she shows us the frontispiece of the *Gone with the Wind* doorway, Mrs. Feltus says, "That's some of the finest millwork you'll see in the South."

Mrs. Jane Conner purchased the home in 1849. A widow, she set up housekeeping with thirteen children. She built the west wing where our rooms are located and a private school for her children, which we can see from our porch.

"A lot of the furniture belonged to Miz Conner. That old 'roller pin' bed in your room?" Mrs. Feltus says to Sharon, "It dates to about 1840." She refers to the large, round, wooden pin that rests at the top of the headboard. "Back when the mattress and comforter were made of feathers resting on rope springs, two servants would roll the pin back and forth on top to smooth the bedding."

Mrs. Feltus's children are the sixth generation of Conners to call Linden home. "We tell everybody we broke Southern tradition. We only had two and not thirteen!"

We all laugh aloud.

"Where does the name 'Linden' come from?" Tom asks.

"It's German; the national tree of Germany."

"Do linden trees grow here?"

"Yes they do." The bark of the linden tree was once used to wrap tobacco, so they were grown as much for their utility as anything. Linden trees still grow on the property today. She explains that, architecturally, Linden was a Federal house.

Tom explains that his ancestors from New England built a Federal-style mansion in Bristol, Rhode Island, in 1810. "It's called Linden Place."

"Is that right?" says Mrs. Feltus.

"The name of your house is definitely one of the draws in coming here."

Mrs. Feltus provides a detailed explanation of the provenance of each piece of Federal and Chippendale furniture and almost every portrait. She explains how the convex mirrors on the walls expanded the light in each room by reflecting the flames in hurricane lamps. The light is also picked up in the gloss of the intricate framed silk embroideries hanging on the walls. She demonstrates the "jib" window: wall panels beneath some windows open to create a doorway when the panes are raised. This is another architectural feature designed to cool the house. In the parlor, she points out the cottage grand piano built by Broadwood and Sons of London. "It dates from 1830. It has a wonderful tone. Does anybody play?" She looks at us with raised eyebrows.

"Regrettably, nothing more than 'Chopsticks,'" says Sharon.

We learn about syllabub, a dessert made with whipped cream, rum, and other liquor. "They say it got its name from the fact that if you ate more than one you could not say your syllables."

"I wish I could taste some," says Sharon.

"I'm sure you would enjoy it," says Mrs. Feltus.

"By 1890, Linden had forty-six acres. It originally had one hundred and fifty. Today I have seven, and that is *ample*." Mrs. Feltus's tone and wry sense of humor keep us smiling or laughing throughout the tour.

She pauses at a map of the grounds and points out buildings that no longer exist. They include servants' quarters, a kitchen, dairy, outhouse, shotgun bowling alley with one lane, and billiard room.

We are surprised at her revelation that the agricultural plantations did not adjoin the houses in Natchez. "These were their *town* houses," she explains. "Their plantations were out in the country or across the river. Most had plantations on both sides of the Mississippi, similar to New Orleans. The French Quarter was originally town houses for sugar and rice planters along the river. They would go into New Orleans in the social season or whatever the occasion might be. In Natchez, there was so much property that they could build even bigger houses, like Linden."

"I'll tell y'all somethin' funny," she continues. "When I came here as a bride, 'cause I wasn't born and reared here, my husband said, 'I wanna tell you somethin'. First of all, you don't ever remember anybody's name, so call everybody honey and darlin'"—and I'm still doin' it. And the second thing he said was, 'Don't gossip about anybody that you meet because we're all related.' And he's not kiddin'. We are."

Tom shares that, during our visit to Gamaliel, "It seemed like everybody I met had a name that's related by marriage to my grandfather's family."

"Oh, yeah! That's what I'm talkin' about," says Mrs. Feltus.

As our entertaining tour concludes, Tom says, "I'd like to ask kind of an indelicate question, if I may."

"Okay," our hostess replies.

"Are there many black people that come and stay here?"

She does not hesitate. "No, and it isn't that they're not allowed to. If they book a room, I don't ask anybody what color they are. I don't ask if they're Mexican, American, Spanish, or anything else. It's open to all people. They've never been turned away from any of our homes."

She pauses a moment. "I'm eighty years old. I don't approve of slavery and there's still slavery in other countries today. It's not right for one human to own another. But, no, we probably get along better with them than anybody else in the United States."

Tom says, "I have friends who say racism in the North is often worse there than in the South."

"Oh, it is . . ." Mrs. Feltus interjects.

Tom continues. " . . . because it's so deceptive."

Mrs. Feltus explains how white and black people are used to living together in the South. She admits they have lived on different social and economic "planes" but that they're all getting closer to living on the same plane. There are economic differences regardless of race and differences that separate people of the same race.

She tells us her family enjoys good relationships with all of Linden's employees and she's found she does better with black employees than white. They share meals together. According to her, things are more open now and even more so with her children. She illustrates with a story about Sherwood, the black man who has been working outside the house during our tour. His cousin Walter worked for the Feltus family for many years. When Walter died, Mrs. Feltus was in Hawaii and couldn't get home for the funeral. She called the funeral home and asked that they drive Walter by the house en route to the church. She wanted Walter to pass by Linden "'cause he'd been such a wonderful friend and employee. After my husband died, he'd come over and sit the house and I'd call and say, 'Walter, you can go home.' 'No, ma'am, I'm gonna stay here until you get here and when you get in safely, then I'm goin' home.' Well you can't find that devotion from a lot of people."

Mrs. Feltus paid for Walter's funeral. "That doesn't mean I'm a great person. I owed it to him. I sent some of his children to college."

"So it feels to you like things are changing, even in the Deep South, as generations come along?" Tom asks.

"Well I think they are," she replies. "We've changed better here than damn near anywhere else; 'course I guess we had a longer way to go."

We hand her our business card and tell her about our book.

She says, "Oh, good! I just can't wait till it comes out. Let me know, okay? I'm glad you asked because I don't mind discussing it at all."

"We appreciate that very much," says Sharon.

"You'll find most people don't mind."

"I was curious because my family were slaves," says Sharon. "So sleeping in a plantation house—I really wanted to do this. I wanted to see it from this side and I got a real education on the furniture and art."

Mrs. Feltus answers, "We just don't discriminate, and I don't know many people who do, against any race." She goes on to explain the reason Natchez has more antebellum structures than anywhere else in the United States; "During the war, Northern soldiers only burned down two buildings. Most people lost their property because of the scalawags comin' in here making use of the nation defeated. That's just the way it was. They lost their way of life. I'm not sayin' it was right or wrong. I'm just saying they lost it."

After the war, all the former plantation owners had left were their townhouses. "They might've had a leak in the ceiling they couldn't afford to fix. They'd pull out their grandmother's silver punch bowl to catch the leak. But they wouldn't sell the punch bowl to fix it. That's why the homes in Natchez have so many original furnishings.

"And when you saw in *Gone with the Wind* her eating that potato in the garden when she went back to Tara? That's not far from the truth either. Dr. Nutt [the owner of Longwood, another antebellum home in Natchez], who had $10 million before the war, was begging for food before it was over."

She then explains that slavery wasn't the only reason behind the war. "It was also economics. The big manufacturers in the North were moving to the South. Paid labor was cheaper, not to mention slave labor. And they could operate almost year-round because the weather was warmer. And they used freeing the slaves as probably a little sideline. I'm not saying they weren't absolutely 101 percent right to free people regardless. That was good. But it was not just that. The northerners weren't that good of a Samaritan, I can guarantee you."

We chuckle.

"Can you imagine what they did to their people who worked in their factories up there?" she asks.

"Well, yeah," says Sharon, "I mean, there are some horror stories."

"I would have rather been a slave on a Southern plantation than work in those factories, I'm gonna tell you right now. I do know that some of the slaves were mistreated. I don't deny that. I know they were. But I'm gonna tell you this: When you go buy a car and you pay thirty thousand dollars for a car, do you come home and get a stick and beat the hell out of it? No! Slaves were property whether we like it or not. They paid money, five, eight thousand dollars a slave. And they were gonna take good care of their slaves, just like in *Gone with the Wind*. They took care of the people on their place. They had doctors. They made sure they had food. They didn't have the finest clothes but there were clothes, and in winter they were warm because they had stoves, and, you know, they weren't fancy, but they had ways to heat their cabins.

"Most of the mistreatment of the slaves was done by overseers, not by the owners. There was many an overseer that was fired, sent walking, because of that. But you don't hear about all of that. And I'm not taking up for the plantation system at all, because it was wrong. But they were better treated than your people who worked in the factories up north because up there the owner of the factory didn't care if they had heat at home or not or if they ate or not as long as they were at work.

"The only thing that is gonna save all of us is to get our economics straight here in the States. And it has nothing to do with Obama; it was there when he got there. The color of his skin has nothing to do with it. Bush was probably the worst president we've ever had. His father bought that for him. His brother would have been a much better president," she tells us.

"Let me tell you something. You know why he didn't run? He married a Mexican. Does that show you what we're talking about? He's smart. George Bush didn't have enough sense to get out of the rain."

After a prolonged goodbye, we load our bags into the Jeep and make our way across the swollen Mississippi into Louisiana.

LIFE ON THE PLANTATION

Twenty miles across the state line we arrive at Frogmore Plantation, an eighteen-hundred-acre working cotton farm. The owners have restored eighteen structures that date from the early nineteenth century as well as a rare, steam-powered cotton gin. This was another of Sharon's must-sees. Having spent the night in a town home, we will now experience a plantation.

Our tour begins in a rustic cabin that once housed enslaved people. Our guide turns on an introductory video. We learn that there is an average of twenty-eight seeds in each boll of cotton. Before the cotton gin was invented in 1793, automating the separation of seeds from the cotton fiber, it took one person an entire day to remove the seeds from just one pound of cotton. During the day, everybody picked cotton. One person could pick 250 pounds or more per day. In the evenings, women and children picked out the seeds. The cotton gin significantly affected production and income, and produced a concomitant demand for more slaves.

The present-day owner of Frogmore, Lynette Tanner, looks out at us from the video: "It's inconceivable to us that the institution of slavery ever existed, but we have to remember that, at this point in our history, nearly every nation in the world was a slave-owning country and, regrettably, it still goes on today."

She points out that only 25 percent of southerners owned slaves. Only 1 percent owned more than one hundred people. Ninety-four percent of Africans were not brought to America but taken to South America and the Caribbean.

Within this narrative is a familiar refrain. We have encountered several southerners who, while not defending slavery, try to deflect blame and defend certain aspects of antebellum life. Tanner quotes a woman interviewed for the Federal Writers' Project in the 1930s who complains that the end of slavery left her with a hungry belly and nowhere to live. She seems to balance things by quoting a man who said slavery was a bad thing and freedom meant no one could whip him anymore. She then reads a claim that, within two years of the end of the Civil War, two out of three slaves wished they were back with their masters.

After the video concludes, the first stop on our walking tour is the smokehouse. "The slaves were very creative with hogs," says our guide, Melissa. "Nothing was wasted." (The choice cuts went to the white people in the big house.) She explains how food was produced and preserved. Life for everyone improved beginning in 1795 when canning was invented by the French. Fruit and vegetables could then be preserved for extended periods of time.

Melissa points to a book on the shelf: *Plantation Mistress* by Catherine Clinton. She says, "They came to realize that life was not quite like *Gone with the Wind*. One of the hardest workers on the plantation, other than the slaves, of course, was the owner's wife. She could totally run the farm without her husband."

We entered a typical slave cabin, where an average of five to seven people lived. Built around 1840, it became a sharecropper's cabin after the Civil War. The shingled roof and ceiling rafters are original. The simple structure features a fireplace that served two adjoining rooms. Individual vegetable gardens were just outside and could be tended during off hours.

One of our fellow visitors asks if a family would occupy one cabin.

"This is my personal explanation," says Melissa. "I don't use the word 'family' with slaves. For one thing, they're not kidnapped, stuck in the bottom of a ship, and brought over here on a three-month voyage with their families, okay? It was illegal for slaves to marry, but they did perform little ceremonies like 'jumping the broom.' If they did have a so-called family—a husband, wife, and children—they would have their own cabin and that may be half of this one. Ordinarily, I think it was more communal-style living; a fifty-year-old man, a fourteen-year-old girl, some others, all living in the same cabin."

She points out Robert William Fogel's *Time on the Cross* and says, "Now this is an excellent book. It will answer most questions that you have about slavery. Robert Fogel won the Nobel Prize in Economic Sciences. He studied actual plantation records. He gets into why the South had slaves, what they ate, what they wore, their treatment, how many bales per acre they could pick, why slaves weren't paid."

Sharon shakes her hand in front of her body.

"You don't like it?" asks Melissa.

"No, no, my arm hurts," says Sharon.

"I thought you were going, 'nah, I don't think so . . . '"

"No, I fractured my arm so I need to move it around," Sharon explains. Everyone laughs.

"When sharecropping began after the Civil War, black people had to come up with their own food, clothing, and shelter. There was not a lot of that after the war, so it meant charging what you needed to live at the plantation general store against the share of the crop you would get at the end of the season. Most people never got out of debt. Their former master, if he survived the war, could be an amputee. His sons might not have survived. His home might have been burned to the ground. He had no land, no assets, and no labor. He couldn't borrow money. It was hard times for all. No one ever got rich off of sharecropping; black or white. Then you had a few droughts, a few floods, and the Great Depression.

"When the plantation flooded, which it regularly did before levies were built, the owner would go to his townhouse in Natchez and the slaves would camp out up in the hills until the flood receded."

"It wasn't a good time to be living," someone in our group says.

"Oh, I don't know," says the guide. "Our prisons weren't overflowing. We didn't have drug problems, and we were eating good food out of the garden."

Sharon wants to know, "Were the people here known to be fair? A lot of the sharecropper plantations were not. People got cheated a lot."

"I think they were," Melissa responds. "From what I know, the thing with sharecropping is, if it wasn't fair, people would just move on. I've had several people over the years stop by whose families worked here and from what I've learned, it was."

We move on. The washhouse and sewing cabin include a loom, quilting rack, nineteenth-century washing machine, and washboards. Melissa tells how slaves could weave two or three yards of coarse "slave cloth" per day. This is the cloth out of which their clothing was made. A few yards from the cotton field stands a three-hole privy that our guide informs us no longer functions. The pigeon house is no longer in use either. A wood-fired oven sits outside the cookhouse, which is where people gathered for meals. "What we call Southern cooking is African. We got many contributions from the slaves, not just in our fields."

From the overseer's cabin, we look out over a vast expanse of field: hundreds of acres designated for planting. During much of the year, visitors can pick cotton. We happen to be here at a time when the plants have not matured enough to allow that.

"Your job," our guide continues, "the amount of cotton you were expected to pick, is according to what you can do, and always more was expected, I'm sure. Your incentive was not to be punished, number one, and you might get some kind of reward; maybe a little whiskey, a little tobacco, maybe a little money; but the slave didn't need money. He couldn't go to town, so what was the point? Slaves didn't have a lot of possessions.

"The only people that equaled and passed the slave as far as what they could produce were the Germans. Robert Fogel gets into that in his book."

"The Germans would've had the incentive," says Tom, "that they would benefit from the fruits of their labor."

"Exactly," says Melissa.

We later learn that Fogel's book is highly controversial. He and his writing partner drew conclusions from very small samples and generalized for the entire South. Yet we ran across several tour guides who recommend it highly.

As we discuss the chapel, constructed specifically for use by slaves, Melissa tells us, "Slaves far outnumbered white people, and whites lived in constant fear of them. Their ultimate thought is freedom. This is why they weren't educated, so they couldn't communicate. They cook your food. They can poison you. They can burn your house down and kill your children. So you want to keep an eye on their free time and maintain social order. What better way to do that than to have a Sunday service that says 'obey your master'?"

We pass a barn and sugarcane mill, both filled with supplies and tools from bygone days. We walk toward the building that houses a steam-powered gin constructed in the 1880s that could produce one to three bales of cotton per day. By contrast, the computerized gin at Frogmore today can produce nine hundred bales per day.

From the loading dock outside the barn, bales of cotton were once carried across the road to a shallow, muddy river full of alligators and frogs. Workers launched transport boats into the river using long wooden poles and navigated seven miles to the landing where three rivers meet. There, cotton was loaded onto steamboats and transported down the Black, Red, and Mississippi Rivers to New Orleans. The raw cotton was sold to merchants in England and textile mills in New England.

"What a process," says Tom. "Are there still frogs and alligators over there?"

After assuring Tom that the natural food chain was still in order,

Melissa explains the different grades of cotton, ranked according to ranges of "middling" (good middling, strict middling, low middling, and so on). It is from these variations that people answer the question "How are you today?" with a response of "Oh, fair to middlin'."

Included in the obscure trivia that appeals to both of us is learning that Crisco, the cooking product with which people have baked for generations without knowing what it is, is the acronym for "crystallized cottonseed oil." Sharon informs Tom later that an infusion of cotton-root bark was used by enslaved women as a method of birth control, inducing abortion.

The tour ends in the gift shop that was once the general store for the sharecroppers. The shelves include books on life during slavery and Jim Crow: *Uncle Tom's Cabin*, *Frederick Douglass on Slavery and the Civil War*, and many others. We're pleased to see they have a variety of books dealing with issues of race. Sharon buys a copy of *Little Black Sambo*, described in this modern reprint as a hero.

We talk further with Melissa, thanking her for her candor. At both Linden and Frogmore, the owners and staff were quite willing to discuss complicated and challenging issues. Though we take issue with some of their information and conclusions, we appreciate their willingness to talk about it.

NUTT'S FOLLY

Both Mrs. Feltus and Melissa recommended that we tour Longwood; another antebellum home in Natchez. They said it was the most popular tour of all the houses, and we wouldn't be disappointed. We decide to wrap up our day there.

A huge structure looms before us at the end of a long, winding driveway. As we crane our necks to take it all in, we know we have not been steered wrong. The house *is* unique. Unlike the Greek Revival style so popular in the South during the mid-to-late nineteenth century, Longwood is an octagonal, six-story Oriental Revival–style house of thirty thousand square feet, topped by a Byzantine dome.

We wait in the gift shop for our tour to begin. There are books on Southern cooking and gardening, John Kennedy Toole's *A Confederacy of Dunces,* and a book with the intriguing title *Someday You'll Thank Me for This: The Official Southern Ladies' Guide to Being a "Perfect" Mother.* Sharon gets a good chuckle out of that one.

Two books really catch our attention. Prominently displayed, with the Confederate flag gracing the covers of both, are *The South Was Right!* and *Southern by the Grace of God.* We glance at each other with a look that says, "What have we gotten ourselves into?" We surmise that this tour may be a little different from the other two we experienced today.

The South Was Right!, written in 1994 by the Kennedy twins— Ron and Donnie—is described on the authors' website as "an authoritative and documented study of the mythology behind Civil War history and its lasting effects on contemporary society." The book "uncovers evidence that the South was an independent country invaded, captured, and occupied by a vicious aggressor."

The Amazon product description of *Southern by the Grace of God,* written by Michael Grissom, reads, "Just when you thought the liberal press had succeeded in grinding us into the ground with their barrage of derogatory patter, a glimmer of hope emerges, and southerners are once again discovering that being Southern is a good thing after all—just like it used to be!"

According to the Southern Poverty Law Center, the authors of both books are prominent members of the League of the South, a white supremacist group. Grissom is also a member of the Council of Conservative Citizens.[1]

When it's time for the tour to begin, a young man invites the dozen or more of us who have been waiting to pass through a door at the side of the gift shop. We emerge into a large, well-appointed room filled with— what else?!!—antique furnishings. "My name is Jack [not his real name] and I'm glad I'm going to be your guide today. Welcome to Longwood." Jack appears to be about eighteen years old. He notes that this is the largest octagonal house in the United States, and that we are standing in its basement.

Jack explains the types of furnishings, construction materials, and other features. Architect Samuel Sloan was commissioned by the owner, Haller Nutt, to build the house that would come to be known as "Nutt's Folly." Construction began in 1860. Sloan, from Philadelphia, brought seventy-five workmen with him. In eighteen months they laid approximately 750,000 bricks. When news of the Civil War came, the men dropped what they were doing, set down their tools and returned to Philadelphia. Haller Nutt pressed on after the mutiny by hiring local workers to patch the walls and roof together enough so his family could move into the basement. This area was more than adequate living quarters for a big family. Nutt thought the war would not last more than a few months. He believed the South would win. The changing tide of war precluded further construction. The house was never completed.

We enter the master bedroom. Its walls are adorned with portraits of Haller Nutt, his wife, Julia Williams Nutt—who gave birth to eleven children—and other family members. Jack points out Julia's "multi-purpose chair" next to the bed: a resting chair with a built-in chamber pot. After Jack identifies the family members in the various portraits, one remains that he has not mentioned.

"Who is the black guy up there?" Sharon asks.

"That is Uncle Frederick," Jack replies. "Uncle Frederick was born into slavery and plays an important role in this house. His job was to be Haller Nutt's playmate. He also became Haller Nutt's closest friend. When he became a free man before the Civil War started, he moved into this house with the rest of the family."

"How did he become free before the Civil War?" Sharon presses.

"I have no idea," says Jack. "He probably bought his freedom." He explains that Haller's father was one of the wealthiest cotton planters in Mississippi, so Haller probably helped him buy his freedom. Jack reiterates their close friendship and shares the fact that Uncle Frederick is buried in the family cemetery right here on the property.

"Where's the cemetery?" asks Sharon.

"I'll show you at the end of the tour," says Jack. "What's really surprising about Uncle Frederick is that in no other house will you see a servant dressed as he is."

"Or a portrait of them," Sharon offers.

"Or a portrait of them in their bedroom," repeats Jack.

This isn't the first or last of Jack's stories that will strike us as a bit odd.

"Nutt lost all of his crops. He lost everything except the building on his Louisiana plantation winter quarters. He died soon after, leaving his family to live in the basement of Longwood for two more generations.

Julia lived here for the next thirty-three years until she died at age seventy-five."

"How were they able to survive after that?" someone asks.

"Uncle Frederick," says Jack with emphasis.

Jack repeats that, even though Uncle Frederick was born into slavery, he became Haller Nutt's best friend. It's because of him that the family survived. Julia didn't know anything about plantations. After the death of her husband and the ravages of the Civil War, she didn't have a clue about how to plant, plow, pick, or sell. All of Nutt's property in Louisiana was seized by the government after the war when property taxes increased. Julia could not pay them. Uncle Frederick moved in and saved the day.

"Now, imagine this," Jack says. "You go from having forty-nine thousand acres of land . . ."

"Is *that* how much land there was?" Sharon exclaims.

"Yes, in Louisiana."

"Forty-nine *thousand* acres," she repeats, astonished.

" . . . acres of land," Jack confirms. "Then in an instant, it's gone and she's down to ninety acres here in Natchez. She went from having the world to nothing at all."

Tom looks at Sharon. She smirks and rolls her eyes.

Later in the tour, Jack points toward a chair and says it is one of the most interesting things about Haller Nutt. This is the chair in which he would rest after working with his slaves out in the fields. He would assist in planting the crops, picking the crops, and baling the cotton, all of which made him suffer from gout in his feet (acute inflammatory arthritis, which is very painful and causes swelling). He sat in this chair to relieve his discomfort.

"Nowadays, we have a way of pulling out the fluid, but back then, you just had to sit and wait until the swelling went down. What Haller did is make himself an early recliner. That is Haller Nutt's gout chair."

Sharon smirks again.

The rest of the tour takes us through the unfinished upstairs area. It is easy to imagine what might have been in this elaborately designed six-story structure had it been finished. One room is filled with 150-year-old tools abandoned by the Philadelphia workers when they fled north.

Tom's Story

Our tour ends at the top of the steps of a large, outside porch. I approach Jack and hand him our card. "My partner and I are writing a book. That's why we're visiting places like this."

"Oh, you're writing a book about all the history," Jack says.

" . . . and the impact issues of race continue to have," I explain.

"Well this house actually contains no racial . . ."

"Except for the man who saved the family," I interrupt and laugh.

"Well, nobody in the family was racist who lived in this house," is Jack's emphatic reply. "Since Haller's best friend was a black man, he was not a racist man at all, and he . . ."

"But how could you own your best friend?" Sharon interjects.

"He *did not* own his best friend," says Jack, beginning to look alarmed.

"But that's what you said," Sharon responds. "He was his slave."

"No, he was *not* Haller's slave. His job as a servant when he was born into slavery was to be Haller's best friend." He continues, "Well, it was to be his playmate, and, as they grew up, Haller did not own Uncle Frederick. He became Uncle Frederick's best friend."

"He paid to get himself out?" Sharon asks.

"Well, no . . ." Jack smiles in frustration and chuckles. "You're taking the words out of my mouth, okay? You're rearranging my words. Now, he was not owned by this family. If he was owned by this family, then the family set him free. But they did not treat him as if they owned him. They did not treat any of their slaves as if they owned them. Most houses here in the South, they would beat their slaves on a regular basis just to make sure they would work for a low wage. Haller would go out in the field and work with his slaves and he didn't pay them a minor wage. He paid them above the normal wages that a slave or a servant would be paid."

"The definition of slavery is that you don't get wages," says Sharon.

"Well, he paid them more than a normal slave would get paid."

"But slaves don't *get* paid," Sharon insists. "That's why you're called a slave. It's *free* labor."

"Well, servant . . ." Jack offers.

"And the servants were also slaves," Sharon says, not backing down, "which is also free labor. You gotta read that part of the history."

"I'm still reading the history book," Jack replied. "So . . ."

"Are you in school?" I ask.

"I'm going to college this fall."

"What year will you be?"

"Freshman."

"All right," I say, trying to be nice. "You're doing good work here."

"Thank you," says Jack.

"Yeah," says Sharon, "we just need to tune up that story just a little bit."

"Okay . . ."

"There's always more to it," I say, "It's deeper than . . ."

"Well, make sure *you* read the history books and everything before you write . . ."

"I *do* read the books," says Sharon. "That's why I'm saying this, okay? My family members *were* slaves, so it means a lot to me that you get *your* story straight."

A woman sitting on a stone wall nearby has been listening to our conversation. She says to no one in particular, "The slave quarters back here were nice."

"Yes they were," Jack agrees, "very nice."

He turns back to us, clasps his hands together and announces, "So I'm going to go help close up the shop."

"Okay," says Tom. "Thank you very much."

Jack almost runs into the gift shop.

"Those slave quarters are very nice," the woman says again.

"We'll go check them out," says Tom. We walk away toward the former slave quarters. They've been redesigned for use as bathrooms and a photo display gallery. There's nothing to indicate that there is anything original about them or what they would have been used for in the past.

Sharon says, "Sorry. I was doing really well until . . ."

"Yeah, I might normally feel a little badly for someone like Jack with us ganging up on him. He's young. He doesn't know. But good grief! This place hires him and he tells this crap to lots of people every day."

We later read, in William Kauffman Scarborough's *Masters of the Big House: Elite Slaveholders of the Mid-Nineteenth-Century South:*

[Haller Nutt] routinely punished slave offenders by placing them in chains or incarcerating them in stocks, and he hired professional slave catchers to track his runaways with dogs. On one occasion, after finding conditions on one of his plantations in a deplorable state, not only did the angry proprietor berate the overseer for running out of pork, but he whipped "nearly all the negroes."

Sharon's Story

The slave quarters were nice?!!
Slaves were handsomely paid servants?!!
Frederick was the slave owner's best friend?!!
Give me a break!

It makes me sick to see how so many white people are devoted to finding ways to absolve themselves. Most of the time, they maintain stoic silence, but then pass these untruths on to their children? And in this case, to God knows how many tourists each week.

Jack is a virtual child, an eighteen-year-old boy. He has learned to interpret the truth in a way that lets his ancestors, and him by default, off the hook for any culpability. He is telling me *I* should read the history books so I can get *my* story straight?!!

FORKS OF THE ROAD

Our last stop in Natchez is the Forks of the Road. This spot was the second-largest slave-trading market in the United States after New Orleans. Pulling off the busy street is challenging. Our destination on this well-traveled thoroughfare is where three roads meet. It is easy to see why it was chosen as the location for a slave market. Yet, it is so unassuming we almost missed it. Once again, the three roads at the intersection include one named Liberty.

From the 1830s until 1863, the spot where we stand is where thousands of people were bought and sold. Black men were dressed in top hats and clean suits; poked and prodded like cattle; and paraded before crowds, their bellies stuffed with fattening victuals and their skin greased to appear healthy. Black women were evaluated for strength and childbearing prospects.

CHAPTER ELEVEN

Truth Be Told

Traveling in the close confines of a car for thousands of miles with someone you have not known long is not easy. We had made a commitment we were determined to keep. After several shorter trips together, we were confident we could endure longer stretches as we dug more deeply into history and healing. Our excursion to Tobago confirmed that being together in historically significant places provided perfect inspiration. Our extended road trip capitalized on that lesson.

We developed an arduous schedule that would take us over almost half of America, into the heartlands and heartaches of history. We tried to balance that schedule so each of us would be satisfied with experiences that touched on our personal genealogies while allowing us to bear witness to historic trauma. We factored in "time-outs" for pleasurable opportunities to enjoy local cuisine and music. In the end, we cobbled together an itinerary we doubted anyone else we knew had tried to achieve.

Given all the places we both wanted to visit, we started off planning two separate expeditions. The first would last approximately a month and take us through the Deep South and Midwest. The second would last ten days and take us to Virginia, Washington, DC, and locations in the Northeast. Tom wasn't excited about flying back East twice; Sharon didn't want to be away from home for six weeks straight. We discussed destinations we could delete, and reduced our time on the road to a total of four weeks. Covering twenty-one states in less than a month was more than ambitious, but felt indispensable to achieving our goals.

The exercise meant engaging in a lot of compromise and sacrifice just in the planning. Once on the road, it was often a challenge to agree where we wanted to eat on any given day. We ended up at so many Subways and Chinese buffets that neither of us may ever touch a fast-food sandwich or pot-sticker again. We became addicted to Dairy Queen ice cream desserts.

There was also the matter of accommodations. Tom's resourcefulness resulted in a system that enabled us to book motel reservations online at the last minute, which saved substantial funds. He found places where Nemo was accepted without charge. Red Roof Inns became our friend. With rare exceptions, this is where we rested our weary bones.

Beyond food and beds, there were bigger, more meaningful decisions. Tom didn't want to sleep in a slaveholder's house in Natchez. But we did, and it was one of our best experiences. Sharon didn't want to leave Nemo overnight at an unknown vet. But she did, and it worked out fine. All along the way, we somehow worked things out.

Our single blow-up occurred in Brookhaven, Mississippi. In spite of our best efforts to make compromises, to be coherent and reasonable, things exploded. There was nothing significant about the place. We were at a Super 8 in the middle of an empty field bounded by the interstate highway. It was such an odd location that we asked about it at the check-in desk. The clerk explained that the hotel had been built in anticipation of a greater development plan by the city for the area surrounding the highway. The plan never materialized. That left the motel stuck in the middle of nowhere. We were miles removed from our next stop and light-years away from our real lives.

Tom wanted to keep the schedule. Sharon wanted to go home.

Sharon's Story

I am so sick of Tom. I have felt manipulated since the very beginning. He wants to visit every civil rights memorial on earth. I find that redundant. Tom has an agenda I don't share. He wants what he wants and maneuvers his way into getting it. I am tired of compromising. I am tired of being on the road. I think we need to divide this trip up—go home and try again later. I have seen enough. There are too many emotions swirling around in my head. What the hell am I doing on the road with this white man trying to heal, anyway? It's hopeless. I want to go to my nest and regroup.

Tom's Story

Sharon keeps changing her mind. It drives me crazy. I don't know what her agenda is, but it's sure different from mine. I keep acquiescing to her desires. I'm so tired of it. I reached the end of my patience when she announced she wanted to cancel the three-day layover in Michigan. We agreed to return to Three Rivers for a few days, where we would do nothing but write. We agreed we needed the time to write together. Sharon selected the location. Now she says she wants to get home as soon as possible, that she can't really write on the road. She needs to be home for that. I wonder if this is the end of the road for us—at this hotel in the middle of nowhere.

BATTLE ROYALE

"We keep doing whatever *you* want to do!" Sharon snaps.

"I am truly astounded to hear you say that!" Tom snaps right back, "because that's exactly how I feel about *you!*"

It is clear that we both have bottled up strong feelings. Yet our respective declarations catch us both off-guard. We stop. Things don't escalate further. Perhaps surprisingly, we both remain calm.

Sharon says, "I need to be in my home. This is too much."

"If I would have known you wanted to be finished by June 12 or 13, I would've made reservations to fly home then instead of the 17th. I'm away from my home and family too."

"I only agreed to such a long trip because you were so insistent."

We don't say much else. We agree to think about it overnight and revisit it in the morning.

When we meet again around 10:00 a.m., Tom says, "After I calmed down, I realized it didn't matter whether we had three writing days in Michigan or New York."

"I was shocked when you said you felt I was dictating everything. I felt just the opposite. I really had to stop and think about it."

"Yeah, so did I, and I'm fine with shifting things."

In hindsight, it felt kind of silly. We were both jockeying for position and staking out ground on something that felt important but wasn't worth the argument. That moment was another turning point. We're both strong-willed and even obstinate from time to time. We disagreed strongly. And we both paused at the same moment before we said anything regrettable. It turned out not to be a battle with just each other. It was a battle over ingrained thoughts, feelings, and assumptions.

We retreated to our separate rooms and thought about things from the perspective of the other person. Then we both backed down from our positions and were easily able to resolve the schedule and move forward. Rather than react instinctually, we calmed the "lizards" in our brains and listened.

MONEY AND MADNESS

Ten days into our journey, we drive to Money, Mississippi. Our goal is to explore the places associated with Emmett Till's murder in 1955. This event had such a major impact on American society, we had to include it on our itinerary. Sharon was keenly interested because Emmett Till and his mother lived in Chicago. His murder was one reason given by her family for never visiting the South.

We found the boarded-up, crumbling ruins of Bryant's Grocery at a wide spot in the road some ten miles north of Greenwood. This is where fourteen-year-old Emmett was said to have whistled at the owner's wife, Carolyn Bryant. In retaliation, her husband and his half-brother murdered him for a crime known as "reckless eyeballing." Black men were never to cast their gaze on a white woman, much less whistle at her. Black people were expected to cast their eyes downward when talking to whites.

After the incident in the store, Emmett was dragged from his uncle's house in the dark of night. His mutilated body was dumped in the Tallahatchie River; a seventy-pound fan tied to his neck.

Graphic photos of Emmett's corpse appeared on the front page of the *Chicago Defender* newspaper and in the nationally distributed *Jet* magazine. The images inspired outrage around the world. Many consider this murder to have been the event that catalyzed the American civil rights movement. Tens of thousands of people viewed his horrifically brutalized remains at his funeral in Chicago. A few months later, Rosa Parks refused to give up her seat on a Montgomery bus.

We stand before a building engulfed by ivy. The roof is caved in. A sign tacked on front reads "Private Property: Violators Will Be Prosecuted" in bright red letters. We don't talk. We just stand and stare, thinking our separate thoughts. As we've discovered at other times, bearing witness to historic horror sometimes demands respectful silence.

The terrorists, Roy Bryant and J. W. Milam, were tried for murder but acquitted in record time by an all-white jury. A few months after the trial, they brazenly confessed their guilt in an explosive interview in *Look* magazine. Since they'd already been acquitted, they could not be charged again. They pocketed $4,000 in payment for their sensational public admission.

Just two weeks before our visit, the Mississippi Delta Authority erected the first of twenty-five "Mississippi Freedom Trail" markers. This statewide cultural initiative is designed to highlight sites that played a key role in the civil rights movement. The first is near Bryant's Grocery. It gives the basic history of what happened. That is a good thing, because the building will surely not last much longer. When it falls, nothing tangible will remain to keep Emmett Till's memory alive, at least in this location.

We drive to the site of J. W. Milam's former home, to the building where they got the fan to weigh his body down, and to the edge of the river where his body was dumped. The final stop in our Emmett Till pilgrimage is the abandoned funeral home in Tutwiler where his body was prepared for burial. The undertaker advised Mamie Till Mobley to leave the casket closed because of the state of the corpse. Emmett was identifiable only by a ring—his father's—worn on his middle finger.

THE BIRTH OF THE BLUES

We drive by the famous blues murals painted on the side of a long row of brick buildings around the corner from the funeral home. We visit the grave of Robert Johnson at Little Zion Missionary Baptist Church, between Greenwood and Money, as well as "the crossroads" of Highways 49 and 61 in Clarksdale, where he allegedly sold his soul to the devil in exchange for mastery of the blues. We spend the night at the Shack Up

Inn on Hopson Plantation, where paintings of blues musicians adorn the walls. With all the suffering and horror this region has witnessed, it is no wonder the blues was born in the Mississippi Delta.

THE LITTLE ROCK NINE

From Clarksdale, we make our way west to Little Rock to visit the State Capitol, where the monument to the Little Rock Nine was erected, and Central High School, where those nine African American students were prevented from attending the racially segregated school by Governor Orval Faubus. Local mobs of white people threatened to lynch the students. Troops from the Arkansas National Guard enforced the governor's orders. President Eisenhower intervened in what became one of the most important events in the history of the civil rights movement by sending in federal troops to protect the students and enforce the law promulgated by the 1954 Supreme Court decision in *Brown v. Board of Education*.

At every step along the way, just as we had hoped when we planned our itinerary, we experienced seriously painful moments bearing witness to horrific and oppressive events in our nation's past. Fortunately, we also find moments of humor to balance things out. On our drive from Little Rock to Tulsa, Oklahoma, we pass through a town with the funniest name either of us has ever heard. With no disrespect to the residents of Toad Suck, Arkansas, we have to ask . . . seriously . . . Toad Suck?

We found our answer on the website for the annual "Toad Suck Daze" festival. Long ago, when steamboats traveled up and down the Arkansas River, there were times when the water wasn't deep enough for the boats to negotiate. This was before the use of locks enabled continuous river navigation. While captains and crews awaited better conditions, they bellied up to the bar at the local tavern. Town residents who witnessed their unquenchable thirst claimed, "They suck on the bottle 'til they swell up like toads."

Laughing about Toad Suck kept our spirits elevated for the next 275 miles, all the way to Tulsa.

RIOTS IN THE STREETS

On May 30, 1921, a black man named Dick Rowland entered an elevator operated by a white woman, Sarah Page, in the Drexel Building in Tulsa. What happened next is known only to Rowland and Page. One version is the elevator jerked, and they stumbled into each other. Another version is Rowland stepped on Page's foot; she lost her balance and Rowland reached out to prevent her from falling. What is known is that Page screamed. Rowland ran out of the elevator and was accused of a sexual attack. White people wanted to lynch him. Black people prepared to defend him. What unfolded over the next two days was one of the most violent and costly incidents of racial violence in US history. Rampaging whites burned the entire black section of town to the ground, killing hundreds and leaving thousands homeless.

What happened in the Greenwood section of Tulsa was not the only incident of this kind. During this period, there was an epidemic of race rioting and lynching. Greenwood and prosperous areas like it—thriving black communities established after Emancipation—were attacked without mercy by angry white mobs. Approximately twenty-five major riots in thirty-six cities occurred during what is known as the "Red Summer of 1919." Thousands of black people were killed from Charleston, South Carolina, to Brisbee, Arizona. Seventy-six black people were lynched. Tulsa was the site of two of the lynchings. Riots in Springfield, Illinois, spurred the creation of the National Association for the Advancement of Colored People (NAACP).[1]

Walking today through the Greenwood section of Tulsa, we can feel the weight of history that has not been healed. Embedded in the sidewalk along Greenwood Avenue and other streets are bronze markers for every building that was destroyed. A total of thirty-five blocks were obliterated in the conflagration. The Greenwood Cultural Center displays photos of survivors and quotes of their memories.

For three-quarters of a century, the story of the Tulsa riot was buried—left out of history books, classrooms, and community conversations. In 1997, the Oklahoma Commission to Study the Race Riot of 1921 was formed. The John Hope Franklin Center for Reconciliation was established to transform the tragedy into a present-day triumph.

John Hope Franklin was the son of a riot survivor. He, his mother, and sister were on their way to Tulsa to join his father when the family received a telegram telling them not to come. It would be more than four years before they were reunited. Franklin grew up to become an internationally acclaimed historian, professor, author, and adviser to presidents.

He is known as the "dean of African American historians" for the many books he wrote and his undying commitment to telling the truth.

The first effort of the center was the creation of John Hope Franklin Reconciliation Park, which was dedicated in October 2010. Sculpture and interpretive signage tell the story of the Greenwood riot and of the role of African American and American Indian people in building Oklahoma.

We are honored to participate in the center's second annual Reconciliation in America Symposium, where we will lead our first workshop together. After introducing the Coming to the Table model and sharing our stories, we invite the audience to tell theirs. A white woman who works with a local historical society speaks of the advantages that European people have over other ethnicities when it comes to studying genealogy.

An African American woman who married a white man shares the conversations they had about how they would raise their children. She wanted to make sure they knew of their African heritage. "Still in this country," she says, "if you have one drop of black blood, you are black." The couple also mutually committed themselves to honoring their children's white heritage. Now, forty years later, her daughter has married a black man. Her son is married to a woman of Czech ancestry. She has brown and white grandchildren and is revisiting her concepts of racial identity.

Another young African American woman from a military family moved around a lot and grew up in diverse communities. Her perceptions growing up were that everyone was equal. She wanted to be color-blind and just go with the flow. Then, in college, she had a professor who told her it was impossible to be color-blind. That was the first time she admitted she had suppressed her own issues of identity because she didn't want to be the black person in class who called attention to issues of race. She discovered her personal disdain for people who told stories that weren't true and realized her need to recover what it meant to be a faithful storyteller, because stories set the minds of young people. When certain things are left out of history books, or are told in biased ways, they paint a falsely positive image of the United States that allows Americans to avoid the truth.

After two powerful days in Tulsa we pack up once again and head north.

JOHN BROWN'S BATTLE

In Lawrence, Kansas, we visit Tom's distant cousins and attend a reenactment of John Brown's Battle of Black Jack, which took place in 1856. It was here that Brown, who later led the unsuccessful raid at Harper's Ferry, Virginia, and was consigned to history at the end of a rope, led an attack on proslavery forces in a precursor to the Civil War. It was the first battle between pro- and anti-slavery forces in Kansas, which entered the Union as a free state in 1861.

Neither of us has ever attended a reenactment. People are dressed in period clothes, play period music, spin wool on handlooms, sell handmade straw brooms, take photographs on vintage cameras, and forge metal tools over a blacksmith's fire. Sharon notices there are no black people in attendance other than her.

The most sobering part of our visit is not the reenactment, but our visit to an African American burial ground on the property owned by Tom's cousin Mary and her husband Rick. We walk deep into the bush to stand in a place of reverence. Like the cemetery we visited together in Lowndes County, Alabama, where we righted the gravestone of Sharon's presumed white ancestor, this cemetery is well tended. Mary speaks of their commitment to treat this hallowed ground with respect.

Sharon's Story

After traversing four states in one day, just thirty-three miles from our destination—Springfield, Illinois—I see the red and blue flashers in the rear view mirror.

"Uh oh," I say to Tom.

Busted!

I was willfully doing eighty in a sixty-five-mile-an-hour zone. My twenty years without a traffic violation record is broken in, of all places, namesake Morgan County. Even the state trooper chuckles at the irony. His amusement does not stop him from writing me a ticket for $135.00.

THE GREAT EMANCIPATOR

Tom's Story

I was born eighty-nine years to the day after Abraham Lincoln died in a too-small bed in a room across the street from Ford's Theater. Consequently, I've always been deeply fascinated by him. I know he wasn't perfect, that freeing the enslaved was secondary to preserving the Union. There are many contradictions in Lincoln, as there are with all great men who have led this country.

I've read so much about him. Yet this was my first visit to Springfield. I'm sure we spent more time at the Lincoln sites than Sharon would have preferred, but I'm grateful that, if that's the case, she didn't mention it.

The Lincoln Museum offers visitors the ability to explore his life from beginning to end. I'm able to reconsider the vast impact he had and continues to have on US history. I learn about events that shaped Lincoln as a child, his exposure to slavery, the horrors of a slave auction when he worked on the Ohio River, his marriage and children, and events leading up to his election in 1860.

The Union Theater features the film *Lincoln's Eyes*, which focuses on the key issues of Lincoln's presidency, especially slavery. The special effects are spectacular, immersing viewers in ways not experienced in normal theaters. *Ghosts of the Library* is a different type of special-effects-laden presentation in which the ghosts of Lincoln and his contemporaries appear and disappear. Holograms of people, objects, and events in history come magically alive and make them appear real.

The inclusion of so much information related to the wounds caused by the legacy of slavery and racism allows visitors the opportunity to see Lincoln and the Civil War in a more complete light. The result is a deeper understanding of Lincoln and the extraordinary obstacles he faced.

As we tour the home he shared with his family for almost twenty years prior to becoming president, we once again encounter knowledgeable, engaging interpreters from the National Park Service. Not one we've encountered throughout our journey has shied away from the many challenging questions we ask.

After spending most of the day at the Lincoln Museum and his home site, we drive to his tomb, which I enter alone while Sharon waits in the car. She's been here before. Standing at the foot of Lincoln's final resting place, I'm glad to be alone. I think about this day, one of my favorites of our journey thus far. I feel deep sadness for all the violence that has dictated events in our nation's history, from wars to terror to assassinations. Then I walk back outside and climb into the car next to Sharon.

"You okay?" she asks.

"Yeah, I am," I sigh.

Sharon's Story

We took pictures in front of one of the exhibits. Me and wax models of Abraham Lincoln, Mary Todd Lincoln, and their kids. Me and wax models of Frederick Douglass and Sojourner Truth. The hands of the likenesses were so real you could almost feel the blood flowing through their fingers.

I was subdued into reverence in the burial chamber. Tears came to my eyes and I felt an almost overwhelming desire to pray.

CHAPTER TWELVE

The Devil's Half Acre

We can feel the end of our adventure approaching. It feels good. Yet there is still a lot to see and do in Virginia, the birthplace of America. We want to understand something about how America came to be, how racism got to be the pervasive factor it is.

Sharon found the Frontier Culture Museum quite by accident. Tom was driving. Sharon saw a billboard on our way into town. She looked it up on the Internet. It turns out to be just a few miles from our hotel.

It isn't busy when we arrive the next morning. In fact, we're the first visitors. A smiling gentleman walks up, introduces himself, and offers us a guided tour. He points to a golf cart in which he will drive us around. We appreciate his offer, since this looks like a pretty big place. We don't have much time, as this was an unanticipated stop and we have appointments at Monticello, some fifty miles away, in just a few hours.

From the outset, we are impressed with this "living" museum. Interpreters wear period clothing handmade from silk and cotton grown on the property. They tend gardens and churn cheese. Livestock includes cows, pigs, and sheep. Many cats roam around.

The museum is divided into two separate areas, designated the Old World and America. The Old World demonstrates rural life in four homelands of early migrants to the American colonies: England, Germany, Ireland, and West Africa. The villages have been either transported or replicated from originals. Visitors are engaged with a combination of interpretive signage and living history demonstrations.

We are thrilled to find this place. It proves to be one of our favorite interpretive centers of the entire journey—with two caveats. The interpreter at the West African Igbo village was not of African descent. Sharon notes that Africa is always lumped together and shrunk down into one country, even though the continent is four times the size of the United States and has far more peoples and languages than Europe. If there is Germany, England, and Ireland, there should be Nigeria, Ghana, and Angola. The other disappointment is the absence of a Native American village, although we are told one is planned. We find it ironic that America's first people are destined to be last.

THE FOUNDATION PRINCIPLE

By the time we arrive in Charlottesville, the day is baking hot. The parking lots are packed. We locate a partially shaded spot where Nemo can rest safely outside the car.

Watching a film about Jefferson and Monticello in advance of taking the tour is a much-welcomed treat. The theater in the visitor's center is air-conditioned. We ride the bus to the house and wait for our tour to begin.

A woman named Mary introduces herself as our guide. Since Tom stands at the front of the line, he walks next to Mary as she leads us toward the house. She asks him where he's from and what brought him such a long way from Oregon. He explains our journey.

"What's the book about?" she asks.

After he tells her, Mary explains that the west lawn is the "nickel view"—the image on the American five-cent coin. "That's an image that really stuck with me when I first started working here." She notes how that side of the house is where Jefferson's slaves and other property were sold after his death.

Mary begins her presentation. "Thomas Jefferson was born in 1743, three miles east of here." She explains that this area was nothing but a frontier at the time. Jefferson inherited this property from his father. When he was twenty-six and still a bachelor, he started working on his home here, but he never lived here for extended periods of time until he retired from public service. After his retirement, Monticello was his main residence for seventeen years, until his death.

"Monticello is a plantation. That doesn't mean 'big house.' What made it a plantation?" she asks.

"Slaves," someone says.

"The slaves and the crops they tended," confirms Mary. "The crops were tobacco and wheat. The slaves worked tirelessly. They provided the skills that made Monticello self-sufficient."

She describes Jefferson's collections, his personal and political life, and his accomplishments, including commissioning the Lewis and Clark expedition, writing the Declaration of Independence, and founding the University of Virginia.

In the sitting room, Mary speaks of Septimia Anne Randolph; Jefferson's granddaughter. She points out a little cupboard made by John Hemings; an enslaved carpenter, to hold Septimia's doll clothes. "They were close," says Mary. When John was sent to Poplar Forest—Jefferson's retreat house in Bedford County—it is said he cried for five miles along the road because he would miss her. "It was complicated; the relationships of the slaves and the family. They were close but still slaves. Jefferson wrote 'all men are created equal' in the Declaration of Independence, but he didn't free his slaves.

"Possibly you've heard of Sally Hemings. She's a young woman who was an enslaved domestic worker here. We believe they had a relationship. He's the father of at least one of her children."

"Why the 'we believe he fathered one child' as opposed to several?" Tom inquires.

A woman standing next to us says, "It could also have been his brother or his nephew who fathered the child."

"And his brother could have been the father of all of his white children too," Tom says. "I mean, if you're using DNA . . ."

"Well," she says, "she got pregnant when she was in Paris as his daughter's companion."

"Right," says Tom, becoming irritated. "I understand that."

She leans toward Tom conspiratorially and whispers, "I figure some 'Frenchie' got her—"

Tom interrupts. "You mean, Thomas Jefferson?"

"No, no," she insists.

"That's a disgusting thought," snaps Sharon, who is standing nearby.

The woman continues to explain her theory. When she realizes neither of us is paying attention, she raises her voice and says dismissively, "You gotta read the history books."

"We have!" Sharon and Tom snap in unison.

Our tone of voice should be a clue to this woman to walk away. She doesn't. She repeats, "It was some Frenchie . . . Jefferson was too much of a snob."

"Yeah," says Tom, "*right*." His comment drips sarcasm. He and Sharon walk away and rejoin the tour, which by now is moving into Jefferson's library.

"He *was!*" she almost shouts after us.

With a knowing glance, Tom and Sharon signal that they will avoid this woman for the rest of the tour. There's no use arguing or listening to her instead of our tour guide.

Sharon's Story

I feel my face turning red with anger. My blood pressure is up. My skin is hot. I want to slap this woman in her mouth.

What she is saying is so incredibly racist and stupid. She can't believe her revered founding father would have sex with a teenaged slave girl and get her pregnant, but she *can* believe that girl would be there for the taking by a French man? She adds insult to injury by expecting me to agree with her. When I won't, she thinks Tom will, because he's white. I seethe through the rest of the tour.

"Now we're in a three-room apartment that was exclusively for Thomas Jefferson," Mary is saying. "This is the book room, his office, and around the corner, his bedchamber. It's not that no one ever came in here, but one came only by invitation."

I can't help but think of Sally Hemings tip-toeing into his room at night at his behest.

"Jefferson's library, at its largest, was 6,700 volumes. After the British burned the Capitol during the War of 1812—which included the Library of Congress—Jefferson sold his collection to the government. The books are still there. He then bought more. The fifteen hundred books at Monticello represent his retirement collection."

Tom's Story

After the tour, I approach our tour guide privately. I didn't want to ask my question in Jefferson's bedchamber with "Ms. Frenchie" in the room. "In Barbara Chase-Riboud's book about Sally Hemings, she says the room above Jefferson's bed was Sally Hemings' bedroom. They don't claim that on these tours though."

"There's nothing written about it."

"But she wrote that the stairway at the foot of Jefferson's bed was removed three months after her book was published."

"Oh, really? When was the book written?"

"In the '70s."

Mary explains that the Thomas Jefferson Foundation, which operates Monticello, didn't really get a grip on slavery and start interpreting it during these tours until sometime in the 1980s. Now, all tour guides include information about slavery at Monticello and the Hemings family in particular. They also have a special tour of Mulberry Row, where enslaved people worked and lived.

Today's tour is better than it was a few years ago, the first time I was here. The Foundation has done a lot of work to set the record straight. Black people are no longer invisible.

Mary says, "You didn't ask me, but I'll tell you about a book I read recently. It's called *Free Some Day,* written by Lucia Stanton. That book tells all we know about the enslaved families."

LIFE ON THE PLANTATION

We join a group of people standing under a tree on the south side of the house. The house tour ran a few minutes long so we're running late, but we only missed a few minutes. Our guide for the outdoor Slavery at Monticello tour, Betsy Gohdes-Baten, is explaining that the only enslaved people Jefferson ever freed were members of the Hemings family. Four of them were likely his children.

Betsy explains that we can follow Jefferson's attitudes toward slavery in his writings. As a young man, he called slavery an "abomination." He said it should be done away with as quickly and expediently as possible. By middle age, he had changed his tune to say that freeing those whose habits have been formed in slavery would be like abandoning children. He compared slavery to holding a wolf by the ear: You can neither safely hold him nor let him go. By the end of his life, he no longer commented on slavery at all. He concluded that it was a problem that another generation must determine the answer to but acknowledged that if something were not done, the country would come to bloodshed. His comments proved prescient. Thirty-five years after his death, the Civil War commenced.

We walk along a narrow road above a string of vegetable gardens. Betsy explains that Mulberry Row, the lane we're walking down, comprised seventeen buildings when Jefferson mapped it for insurance purposes in the 1790s. The insurer required careful documentation of exactly what was being insured. Jefferson provided a detailed map of everything on the mountaintop. His map verified how far apart the buildings were, what they were used for, and what materials they were constructed from. It proved a wonderful resource for archaeologists. In the late 1970s, archaeologists dug out the full length of Mulberry Row and found the remains of the buildings just where Jefferson said they would be.

We are pleased to hear Betsy be forthcoming about Sally Hemings's children. "What we have is this," says Betsy. "DNA links Eston Hemings and Jefferson's family. It is documented that Jefferson was here nine months before Sally is reported to have given birth all six times she is recorded as having given birth. According to the memoirs of Madison Hemings's [one of Sally's sons], Jefferson is their father. In Jefferson's slave rolls there is no differentiation. Sally is listed with her children. There is no father named. All of them are freed. The supposition is that all of these were likely Jefferson's children."

She explains that enslaved people who lived here worked from sunup until sundown, which meant nine-hour days in the winter and fourteen-hour days in the summer, six days a week. At night, they tended their gardens, which provided much of their food. Everyone age ten and older was considered an adult for purposes of work. "If you worked on Sunday, you got paid and were entitled to keep the money. If you sold the pelts of animals you killed, you kept that money. If you sold vegetables, you kept that money as well."

Evidence says Mulberry Row residents spent most of their money on clothing and, of all things, china. When it was excavated, archeologists found buttons and needles, indicating there was a lot of sewing going on. They also found eighty different patterns of china unlike Jefferson's inventory. They found the neck of a fiddle, dominoes and marbles, forks, knives, metal tools, horse-related items, jewelry, coins, a piece of slate with writing on it, and five leads (pencil equivalents). The last item is indication that there were literate people in the enslaved community.

We gather around an area that was once the blacksmith's shop and "nailer." Betsy explains that the nailer is where young boys began their working careers. Once they had a little practice, they were required to make about a thousand nails a day. It was hot work. There were four forges set up, with five young men assigned to each. "The boys ranged in age from ten all the way up to their early twenties. They're pushing each other around and out of the way. Because of a prank, a fight breaks out one hot day in June. Cary, age eighteen, hits Brown, also eighteen, in the back of the head with his hammer and fractures his skull."

What happened next is in Jefferson's correspondence. His son-in-law, Thomas Mann Randolph, was in charge at Monticello. He wrote to Jefferson in Washington and asked what he should do with Cary. Jefferson wrote back and said to sell him. He wanted Cary to disappear and to serve as a lesson that this kind of behavior was completely unacceptable. Jefferson cared less about the price than the distance he was sold away.

Our tour comes to an end. Betsy announces, "All right, you've heard how Jefferson's enslaved community lived, how they were treated, how they had an opportunity to improve their lifestyle by working just as hard as they possibly could or selling things that they made or raised. If you step out of line, you're sold off the plantation. If you ask a favor and it's reasonable, he grants it. And he has special favorites, like the Hemingses.

"What do you think?" she asks us. "What do you think of Jefferson as a slave owner?"

"He was a man of his time," says one.

"Definitely that," says Betsy.

"Well," says another, "I'm not willing to grant that there's a spectrum of slavery that's benign. I couldn't say that, even with Thomas Jefferson. Slavery dehumanized people and said they were property. They had no rights. They had no standing before the law. The Constitution counts them as three-fifths of a person, purely for purposes of levying taxes and apportioning representation in Congress for their owners. Jefferson benefited from that. He lived his whole life with a contradiction. There's a paradox about him, I think. Even if we grant that there are mitigating factors, that he showed favoritism, no slave woman, Sally Hemings included, could have refused to have sex with him. She was property. I wouldn't want to romanticize that relationship."

"Thank you," says Betsy. "That was well said."

Tom says, "It's interesting how some people want to defend our heroes in ways that don't sully me as a white person. We get this warped sense of what's important rather than recognizing the humanity of *all* the people who lived and worked here and suffered here. It feels like you're doing really good work, and I hope the whole Foundation is supportive of your being so forthright, because it's refreshing."

Betsy responds by telling us, "For a while, when I started working here, I had difficulty because of the impersonal way that Jefferson treats the Hemingses versus how fond he is of his white grandchildren. But then, I thought, you know, that's a product of his time. He sees that they're all freed; the ones that survived to become adults. He trains the boys to be carpenters so they had skills. He doesn't show any particular affection toward the females, and it's not clear that he showed affection toward their mother."

The tour ends. We walk to view Jefferson's grave, catch the shuttle there and ride back to the visitor's center. When we return to the car, Nemo is panting and glad to see us. We give him cold water and carry on.

Tom's Story

Colonial Williamsburg is an hour's drive from where we spent the night in Richmond. Among the multitude of historic homes, tours, interpreters, and displays, our highest priority was Great Hopes Plantation. We planned to take in two presentations led by African American interpreters. Unfortunately, both were sold out. We tried to make the best of things and walked to the exhibit anyway. According to the brochure, Great

Hopes "represents African American slave interpretation, carpenters, and working farmers who were not part of huge tobacco plantations, showing what they did and how they lived." Though we're here on a busy summer Saturday, we encounter only one interpreter at one building among the many inside the enclosure; a white woman inside the slave cabin.

At several museums and interpretive centers we have visited, we've heard about the challenge of finding people of color to act as interpreters for exhibits and reenactments of the life of enslaved people. I was so intrigued that I later engaged in a dialogue on Facebook about this issue and received a variety of interesting comments.

One woman of color wrote, "I would strongly discourage any African American from participating in a reenactment as an enslaved human. I wouldn't give anyone the satisfaction of being on display in that way. Many people would visit those places and find satisfaction in seeing that (and not as a learning experience). I don't know that I could become three-fifths of a person for anyone. That's just asking too much. I would stand there in costume and cry for my entire shift. No one would benefit."

An African American man wrote, "There are some things that are not fit for reenactment. How does one do that with any degree of reverence when the experience itself represents one of the worst forms of human debasement? [It's] degradation in the pursuit of profit."

A white man wrote, "It would make about as much sense as having Jews reenact what it was like to be thrown into the ovens."

The conversation became long and rich with many participants. Along the way, someone sent a link to the website of Nicole Moore, an African American historian, consultant, blogger, and "interpreter of slave life." I contacted Nicole to let her know about the unfolding conversation and she joined in.

"I think what people may miss about reenactments and interpretation is that there are two different ways to handle it. What Williamsburg does is first-person interpretation so the visitor gets the experience as if they traveled back in time. Other sites will do a third-person interpretation where you may look the part and do the work but they are explaining and demonstrating to the visitor rather than acting for them. I love what I do because I get to really expose people to a difficult topic but tailor the experience to what they can handle."

We also found a 2011 NPR interview with Greg James, one of the people who portrays an enslaved man at Colonial Williamsburg. When asked by the reporter why he chooses to do the work he does, he said, "I wanted to do that because our ancestors are not able to speak for themselves. And so their voices need to be heard as well."

BACK ON THE ROAD

Our last day on the road will be spent in Richmond, the capital of the Confederate States of America during the Civil War. We drive to Manchester Docks on the James River, which once operated as a significant port in the internal slave trade in the United States. Tom wants to show Sharon the Slave Trail, which he experienced with other Coming to the Table colleagues two years earlier.

Walking from the car to the beginning of the trail, Sharon doesn't say much. She appears disturbed but doesn't say why. Standing before the interpretive sign near the river's edge at the beginning of the trail, she announces she's leaving. She'll wait for Tom in the car. Although she tells him to go ahead, he departs with her. They walk in silence to the Jeep.

Tom's Story

Sharon's discomfort is palpable. She mentions something about the horror of this place—the darkness beneath the canopy of trees, the blood.

When I was here two years ago, it was for a Re-evaluation Counseling workshop in connection with Coming to the Table; the one out of three that Sharon didn't attend. Two of the participants were Cricket White and Tee Turner. Hope in the Cities, the Richmond-headquartered organization they work for, has operated the Walking Through History program since 1993. The organization believes that "participating in the ritualized recognition of historical sites and events can lead to reconciliation between polarized groups or individuals. It is through addressing the historical injustice as an inclusive group made up of descendants of both perpetrators and victims that each group can help in healing itself and the other group." Richmond's historic Slave Trail walk forms the heart of the interpretive experience.

Reverend Sylvester "Tee" Turner is the director of Reconciliation Programs for Hope in the Cities. When I was here two years ago, Tee explained that at one point 50 percent of all income in Richmond was derived from the slave trade. After 1780, Richmond became the leader in the internal slave trade; the number one exporter of enslaved Africans to other American states. In the early 1800s, the demand for labor in Mississippi and Alabama created a bonanza. People were forced along a trail from the ships in Manchester Docks along the James River. They were taken to slave jails to spend the night before being sold at market. This route avoided the indignity of "southern belles" being exposed to the sight and smell of "raw Negroes."

The tour Tee has led many times begins at the tallest monument in Richmond, which stands atop the city's highest hill. It towers over the James River and offers one of the most panoramic views of both the river and the city. The Confederate Soldiers and Sailors Monument is one of many Confederate statues in Richmond. Like in many places throughout the South, this monument commands a place of extreme honor. A Confederate soldier stands seventeen feet high on top of a seventy-three-foot granite column.

We shared dinner with Tee when we were in Tulsa for the John Hope Franklin Symposium. He said, "You may recall that when I do tours of Richmond, I talk about how I never liked that statue. I *really* don't like that statue." He went on to talk about his eventual realization that he had allowed that statue to keep him in bondage.

"We can talk about creating a safe or comfortable space to allow healing to happen, but it's the process. The more you talk the more you are released of that pain. The more you engage the more you understand the 'why' of the pain and the better you understand the challenges of others.

"For example, freeing myself from that bondage of that statue was part of a process. I learned that the statue was built out of grief."

Seventy-five percent of Richmond males between the age of seventeen and fifty fought in the Civil War. More than one-third of them died or were maimed. "Their wives, children, and parents suffered. Their pain and grief were real, just as the pain of black people and American Indians is real. We too often refuse to listen to the story of 'the other.' Listening only to my story is shortsighted. Whether I like the statue or not, it is part of my story as well as the story of everyone else. Until we hear all the stories and see through the eyes of 'the other,' we remain in bondage and removed from the possibility of reconciliation.

"How I saw the statue after that point changed. I see that sucker every day. But when I drive by it on Main Street, I'm not in bondage to it anymore. When I can own *all* the grief, I can move forward."

I think back on my own awareness of what Tee is talking about. I remember two years ago, when we drove to the same parking area where Sharon and I are today. As I looked out at the James River on that day, I could feel the physical connection by water between the spot where we stood and the rocky shore below the Door of No Return at Cape Coast Castle, in Ghana. I was connected to a memory of standing in that place and crying my eyes out, feeling for the first time what it must have felt like for kidnapped African people being taken into oblivion.

People were stripped of their clothing, chained, and herded from the land, culture, smells, and people—everything they'd always known. They were transported to a land where they had no connection. Their very being had been stripped from its soul. They heard different sounds, saw different birds, plants, land, and buildings. This was the end of one journey and the beginning of another—one that lasted the rest of their lives.

Approximately twenty of us joined Tee for the tour; half of African descent and half European. We walked in silence along the trail, heading upstream along the river. Tee asked us to hold our thoughts in silence, to ponder the transatlantic slave trade. We passed dozens of people fishing on the shore. Most were people of color. Several motorized boats floated in the river. From what I could see, everyone on the boats was white. Some people glanced at us and looked away. Others watched us or said hello. A small boy, no more than two years old, attempted to throw a rock in our direction. His mother scolded him and pulled him away. One white man was speaking in a normal tone of voice to his friend who said, "Shhh," and pointed at us. They both fell silent.

After a quarter mile or so, we stopped and turned around. For the walk back, Tee asked that we walk single file, place our hands on the shoulders of the person in front of us, and again walk slowly down the trail. The walk upriver represented the transatlantic slave trade. The walk back represented the internal version; the sale of slaves from Richmond to other states.

This was more disturbing. There were points where the canopy from the trees above was so thick that it became quite dark and felt enclosed. Claustrophobia crept in. I thought about the horror these trees had witnessed. The ground upon which we now walked was soaked in tears, blood, and terror.

Once we were back where we began, Tee asked us to share our feelings. One person felt transformed into nothingness. Another felt stripped of his culture, religion, language, clothing, and shoes. Others talked of rape, beatings, families ripped apart. The experience gave me an entirely new understanding of being "sold down the river." It meant betrayal—watching your child, sibling, or spouse put back on a ship that would sail down the James and never be seen again.

Tee said, "Allow this experience, like other similar experiences, to shape us a little."

Some of us stood alone; others in small groups. We sought and shared comfort.

We next drove to the site of Lumpkin's Slave Jail, the most notorious of the at least thirty-four holding pens in Richmond where enslaved people were held until being auctioned off. Resistant Africans had to be "broken." This is where it was done. They were reduced to a slave mentality, the acquiescent shadow of a person. This is "the Devil's Half Acre."

Mary was an African woman that the owner of this site, Robert Lumpkin, had children with. When he died, he willed his assets to "the mother of my children" because he could not legally will his assets to a slave. How ironic that a black woman would come to own one of the most nefarious locations in Virginia history. After the Civil War, the former jail became a school for freed black children.

The site was only rediscovered recently. Changes in topography over time resulted in the foundation of the site falling fourteen feet below present grade. The jail, located on what is now a valuable piece of real estate, was discovered during excavation for a development project. The entire site was uncovered to verify that this was indeed Lumpkin's Jail. Many artifacts were found to substantiate this and the site was refilled to await funds to restore it properly.

We drove a short distance to the Reconciliation Triangle statue, which is located at the site of Richmond's former slave market. Three hundred thousand kidnapped Africans and their descendants were sold down the river at this very spot. Tee explained there are two identical statues located in Liverpool, England, and Benin, in West Africa. The fifteen-foot-tall bronze sculpture depicts two people embracing, symbolizing apology and reconciliation for slavery. The base of the statue tells the story of the transatlantic slave trade.

When Sharon and I had dinner with Tee in Tulsa, he said, "I don't consider myself having arrived in my own personal healing, although I do understand the power of historical trauma in a way that I'd never given thought to before. When I think of historical trauma, I know you can't solve a problem until you get to the root of it. When you get to the root, you know where you have to start your work. It doesn't mean that the pain goes away instantly or that time is not required in dealing with the pain. It doesn't change the impact of what that trauma created. But I can now identify where it is so I run into fewer walls. I'm better able to visualize things that I was blind to. That's part of the Coming to the Table process: identifying historical trauma."

Sharon's Story

It would be a lie to say that I felt glad to have visited the horrors of the Richmond Slave Trail. What I can say is that it was a profound experience. I have an ancestor who was taken from Virginia as a nine-year-old child. She was transported "down the river" to Mississippi. I don't think she went by boat, but everything on this trail evoked visceral feelings that are more than disquieting.

Tom and I sat in the Reconciliation Circle and talked about all we had experienced. I was glad I relented after my initial revulsion, took a bit of the walk, and ended up here.

I tried to explain to Tom the overwhelming feelings I had when we arrived. It is hard even now to describe them. Like Forks of the Road and the slave market in Charleston that I visited on my own, this is a place drenched in tears and blood. I can literally feel the spirits. Their pain is my pain. I look through the tunnel of time and recoil at the absolute agony of the people who were brought to this place, stripped of their humanity, and reduced to beasts of burden. I would not treat any living creature with such total, conscious, inexcusable evil. I cannot fathom how others who call themselves human beings could do that.

I don't exactly find peace in this place. That is asking too much. What I feel is a pervasive sadness. My body is literally aching, and not from the

The Devil's Half Acre | 187

physical act of walking. After visiting this place, I know that we are on the right path. Racism is so awesome and so ugly, it absolutely must be strangled out of existence. There is no other way to do it than to confront it.

Tom's Story

Sharon's first reaction was startling and sad. There was no attempt at communication, just, "I'm getting the hell out of here. Go on if you want to."

I don't. I want to be with her. I want to listen, to feel. I want to support whatever she's feeling, even though I don't believe I can. From the moment we walk away from the shore of the James River, we speak barely a word until we reach the statue.

We sit on separate benches several yards apart on different sides of the sculpture. We apologize to each other for any pain we have caused through our words. Though it isn't the first time on this journey, this may be the most powerful moment of connection with Sharon that I feel. It's a connection rooted in pain.

PART FOUR

Truth, Mercy, Justice, and Peace

"Traveler, there is no path.
We make the path by walking."

ANTONIO MACHADO, SPANISH POET

CHAPTER THIRTEEN

Ripples on a Pond

Though slavery in the United States became illegal a century and a half ago, we continue to be impacted by its traumatic legacies today. Schools, neighborhoods, and churches are as segregated as ever. Health disparities between black and white people remain significant. African American people are overrepresented in prisons and underrepresented in colleges and corporate boardrooms. Inequity and mistrust along racial lines are systemic throughout American society.

In seeking to acknowledge, understand, and heal these and other persistent wounds of the institution of slavery, the Coming to the Table approach revolves around four key—and interrelated—activities: researching and understanding *history,* making *connections* with others, individual and collective *healing,* and taking ongoing *action.*

As in dealing effectively with any disease, when discussing slavery and its legacies, we must know the history and causes surrounding them to understand how they continue to affect us and to devise the best treatment to achieve a cure.

Making connections with others—establishing genuine, accountable relationships—is only a first step, but it is a big one. It provides a means to work together to understand, from divergent perspectives, how the legacy of slavery has impacted the lives of contemporary people and offers the possibility of moving forward in a new way.

Healing from the historic trauma of slavery and its aftermath is the ultimate goal of Coming to the Table, and taking ongoing action to address the legacy of slavery and sharing the Coming to the Table approach spreads the healing to others.

Of these four stages, taking ongoing action is perhaps the most important for incorporating the healing model into one's life. In our case, the action we chose was to "live the model" and share our story through blogging, public speaking, social networking, and writing this book.

Ours is but one action among many undertaken by our Coming to the Table colleagues. What began in 2006 with a small gathering of two dozen people has grown into a large community of individuals and groups taking different paths toward the same destination: healing.

There are a myriad of groups beyond Coming to the Table that are working for positive change as well, which is good news indeed for those of us who long to see the paradigm of racial inequity overturned. Although it will take a critical mass of people to achieve sustainable solutions, it all begins with individuals who commit to change their lives, impact those around them, and influence the institutions that serve them.

History teaches that every few generations, society experiences upheaval, invariably motivated by the younger generation coming of age. We saw such transformation in action during the 2008 election that propelled Barack Obama into the White House. His campaign inspired one of the largest youth voter turnouts in American history and changed the public face of America, throughout this country and around the world. After Obama's election, pundits, bloggers, and the media posited America's achievement of a post-racial society. Yet, even as many heralded success, other Americans screamed, "I want my country back." An onslaught of racial invective ensued in the public square that has left some quarters of our country more polarized than ever.

Today's youth cannot escape the shadow of racism that has been passed down organically from parents and others who cling to a distorted image of American history, one informed by, and articulated from, a worldview permeated by white privilege. As discussed in chapter 4, these biases and prejudices are so hardwired that most of us have no idea how quickly and automatically they kick in and how enduring they can be.

The only way we will ever come to terms with the truth about what we have inherited is for people of every age to be more fully educated in the history and legacies of our nation and its institutions.

Western societies have meticulously recorded, catalogued, documented and presented history from their point of view. That is one reason they have been so successful in constructing a worldview in which they are ensconced at the center. Other cultures are relegated to the status of afterthoughts, if considered at all. That is a large part of the challenge we face today. As Sharon's uncle once told her, the word *justice* means "just-us."

Most people—young people in particular—do not have firsthand experience of the transformative historical events that inform the society in which we live today. They were neither slaves nor slaveholders. They do not grasp the magnitude of horror associated with that economic system. They were not beaten during civil rights marches and thus may not fully appreciate the value of their voting rights, much less their right to sit anywhere on a bus or train or drink water from a fountain that isn't labeled "white" or "colored." They can go anywhere and do anything they please, whenever they please. They can marry anyone they want.

As a result, many believe racism no longer exists. What they don't recognize is that it is merely not as obvious as it used to be. History and language have been skewed in the minds of many white Americans to be more palatable and less confrontational. A sanitized story is being passed on to yet another generation.

The truth is that the chasm between races remains wide. Relative to people of European descent, people of African descent fall on the negative side of virtually every social indicator we can measure. The authors of "The Cost of Being Black" report that, in 2006, before the economy collapsed, infant mortality rates were 146 percent higher for black babies than white. The lack of health insurance coverage was 42 percent more likely for black people than white. Median income was 55 percent lower, poverty rates 173 percent higher, and unemployment rates were double. The average white American would live five and one-half years longer than the average black American; seven years for men.[1]

The criminal justice system provides a glaring example of the disparities. Its focus on profits exacerbates the problem. The health-care system is no better. Insurers, drug manufacturers, and even many health-care providers prioritize profits over health. In the end, people suffer and the people who suffer most are people of color.

In spite of these dire conditions, there is hope. Times *are* changing. Today, we have a variety of institutions that present American culture in a different light—one that incorporates *all* people who comprise the American mosaic. On our journey, we were pleased to note many serious, thoughtful, and strategic efforts that will contribute to building a more egalitarian American culture.

Jan Jenner, director of the Practice and Training Institute in the Center for Justice and Peacebuilding at EMU, said it best: "We need to celebrate all of our various identities, but we need to celebrate them in an environment that allows everyone to flourish—everyone to be who they are."

THE GREAT AMERICAN NOVEL

In 1996, Pulitzer Prize–winning novelist Jane Smiley, in an essay for *Harper's* magazine about slavery and racism in American literature, wrote, "Ernest Hemingway...once said that all American literature grew out of *Huck Finn*. It undoubtedly would have been better for American literature, and American culture, if our literature had grown out of one of the best-selling novels of all time, another American work of the nineteenth century, *Uncle Tom's Cabin*, which for its portrayal of an array of thoughtful, autonomous, and passionate black characters leaves *Huck Finn* far behind."

Written by Harriet Beecher Stowe in 1852, *Uncle Tom's Cabin* is a novel that exposes the evils of slavery and caused a national sensation. When Stowe met President Lincoln in 1863, he reportedly remarked, "So this is the little lady who made this great war."

The Adventures of Huckleberry Finn, written by Twain in 1884, is honored as one of America's greatest novels. Through its two main characters—a white boy and an enslaved black man—it takes a scathing look at racism and the entrenched attitudes that feed it. Smiley explains, however, that by making racism and slavery a personal matter between two individuals rather than a political and institutional evil, *Huck Finn* fails even where it succeeds, by allowing white people to feel good about getting over their racism without ever actually doing anything about it. "... all you have to do to be a hero is acknowledge that your poor sidekick is human; you don't actually have to act in the interests of his humanity."

When we decided to work together, our commitment was to respect and honor each other's full humanity. We chose to enter—to the best of our ability—each other's lives and worlds with an open-minded sense of curiosity and a commitment to confront unvarnished truths.

Sharon's Story

One good part about people connecting authentically across racial lines is that it grounds them in a relationship that offers a safety net when it gets painful. And it *does* get painful. I have done more crying in the last three years than ever before in my life.

Getting past my aversion to white people requires reaching a high moral ground where I fundamentally change how I think and find the valor to forgive. I'm not ready to let my guard down totally because I feel if I change and society doesn't, I'm putting my life in danger. I am willing to accept individual people, but I still don't have a broad love for everybody. I truly don't know how, or if, I'll ever get there.

Racism these days is often seductively subtle. Black people attend Ivy League universities. We can get jobs that pay handsomely. We live pretty much anywhere we want. We travel on buses, trains, and planes and don't sit in the back unless we want to. People date, fall in love, and marry across racial lines. I cannot deny that there has been a great deal of progress.

The real challenge is that the system is designed to protect the powerful and it feeds on "isms"—racism, classism, sexism—all methods to keep people divided and conquered. Those in power never give it up without a fight. British historian and moralist Lord Acton said in 1887, "Power tends to corrupt, and absolute power corrupts absolutely. Great men are almost always bad men." Abolitionist Frederick Douglass said, thirty years earlier, "Power concedes nothing without a demand. It never did, and it never will ... The limits of tyrants are prescribed by the endurance of those whom they oppress."

In recent times, common people have risen up. Though the "Arab Spring" resulted in regime change in several Middle Eastern nations, protestors suffered violent backlash from those in power. American citizens mobilized "Occupy Wall Street" protests in cities throughout the country, demonstrating against the huge disparity between the obscenely wealthy and the "99 percent." Their example ignited a wave of protests around the world.

These are hopeful signs, but everywhere you look white people remain at the top of the pyramid, or influence those at the top. Throughout Africa and many other countries, leaders, emulating the European model, hold onto power unjustly, manipulate currency, abuse workers, and engage in corruption, just like their former colonizers.

"So Obama becomes a president who perpetuates many oppressive policies initiated by his predecessors," says Tom.

"Right," I say, "That is the price you pay to become the president. You go with the program. There are so many constraints that are structural; no one person can overcome them, no matter how good his intentions."

That thought was echoed when Tom introduced me to Dr. Richard Wing. We met in his office at the church he pastors in Columbus, Ohio. As youth minister at First Christian Church in Pomona, Dick was influential in the evolution of Tom's worldview in the 1960s. He said two things that really hit home.

First, he quoted John 8:32: "You will know the truth, and the truth will set you free." Then he said, "What John didn't say is that the truth will piss you off before it sets you free."

Tom and I can vouch for that!

Second, he said, "What you experience personally will largely not translate to the wider culture. All you will have is your personal story."

He explained that changing as a result of personal breakthroughs is one thing. But for our country to confront its hideous past in the genocide of Native Americans and the enslavement of African Americans is something no one is willing to do.

I noted that there were at least two people in the room who rebelled against that reasoning: me and Tom. We are confronting these issues, experiencing personal breakthroughs as a result, and hoping to influence many others by sharing our experiences with the world.

My expectation on this journey was that we might discover extreme differences between black people and white people. In some ways, I hoped that would be so. It would help make sense of my feeling that there is something pathological about white people that makes them so aggressive and abusive. It didn't turn out that way. On the most basic, human level, there aren't any discernable differences at all. We aren't tigers and bears. We may disagree about politics, religion, or race, but we all seek love and crave acceptance and companionship.

The differences are social constructs. The culture in which we are raised may affect the food we eat or the games we play or the music and sports we like, but our humanity is the same. Travel and technology have brought disparate cultures closer together. Most people live in urban areas or, if they live in rural areas, are not as isolated as in previous generations. Physical boundaries enforced in the past by legally sanctioned segregation have fallen. Today, people interact more, and it is hard to dislike someone you know if that person is someone you value.

Black people have always said we know ourselves *and* we know white people. Our lives depended on it. But white people don't know us. Maybe there is something in that observation. When our experiment began, I think Tom wanted to know me more than I wanted to know him. Now that we know each other, I find Tom to be a pretty likable guy—an upstanding person who shares my principles and moral values.

When I think about what has changed in me because of our journey, what comes to mind are small, personal things. I am more patient. I am not as reticent about being around white people. I've made friends with my next-door neighbors. I have conversations with the lady at the liquor store, the cashier at the grocery store. I bake pies and occasionally take one to the woman at the real estate office. I am less angry and more peaceful.

Genealogy has helped. My ancestors are no longer mysteries. I am a better repository of information for others now that I know beyond doubt, for instance, that every Gavin in Mississippi is related, either by blood or affinity. Our road trip helped that along as I learned a huge amount from those court records we found. In the past, I have tended to return to the same places repeatedly. Broadening our itinerary—visiting museums and memorials and participating in the many tours we did— moved me beyond my frame of reference.

I still have a hard time discussing topics of consequence with white people. Take my next-door neighbor, for instance. He's white. He's a prison guard. What are we going to talk about? We stick to safe topics like the weather, our gardens, our children. We don't talk about his work. If he were to tell me about something ugly he has witnessed, I don't know how I would respond.

In spite of what we learned, it strikes me that, in general, it is white people who need to work with each other. I can't teach them, convince them, or have any impact because they won't listen to me. They are more likely to listen to Tom because he personifies that which is familiar.

"So, Tom, you get to be the representative for the entire white race."

He rolls his eyes and laughs.

Tom's Story

I began this journey with a great deal of hope. I don't know how much Sharon and I thought we would influence or teach each other, but I'm convinced that some part of us wanted to share as well as receive knowledge and enlightenment. I'm grateful for all I've learned from our experiences together. I can't imagine my life now without Sharon in it. What has come as a surprise is that I feel more pessimistic than when we began. I recognize more than ever just how deeply embedded systems of oppression remain.

The absolute terror unleashed on people of color throughout our nation's history is something I've known about, but mostly in the abstract, primarily from books and films. When you *really* pay attention, it gives you a very different perspective. I pause now when I observe people waving flags and declaring the United States the greatest country on earth. Reveling in that glory without taking into account its entirety, including the horrifying and deeply shameful parts, is ignorant. To be blunt, it is clear to me that systems remain in place in the United States that benefit white people and inhibit everybody else.

I believe Reinhold Niebuhr was right when he said that the arc of the moral universe is long but it bends toward justice. The problem is, the arc is too damn long and bends way too slow.

One of the important lessons for me on this journey regards listening. I've always considered myself one who pays attention. I think I'm a good listener. But I've learned how many ways I'm not. There are times I so want to share what I know, that I don't shut up and listen.

As I consider what has changed in my life since working with Sharon,

I'm reminded of something our friend Tee Turner said. Referring to his growth as a result of leading the Slave Trail walks in Richmond, he told us, "I can't ask you to change if I'm not willing to. We are both victims of history. We are both imprisoned by the past. I talk about black people being in maximum-security prison and white people being in minimum-security prison and that's a big difference, but we don't usually talk about the trauma of white people. You can't put us in prison and not imprison yourself. Whatever boundaries and stipulations you put on us to remain in power; you have to change yourself to maintain that order."

It is the boundaries that need to be dismantled. Sharon and I have certainly broken through some brick walls together. I've learned more about myself and the society in which we live. I recognize more clearly than ever before the privilege I possess. I now more readily reach out to folks from the "other side," even when it is painful, awkward, or uncomfortable.

One underlying theme of *Gather at the Table* is the sharing of food. On the one hand, we dished up our histories, experiences, and thoughts in philosophical and allegorical ways as well as in reality. The result made for any number of delicious and enlightening "meals."

On the other hand, we shared *real* food; everything from basic home-cooked meals to culinary extravaganzas. When Sharon visited our home in Oregon, we prepared mostly vegetarian: lots of tofu and fruit smoothies. Sharon observed that, though she is a committed carnivore, she enjoyed what we served, along with learning something about the reasons we eat as we do.

In Sharon's upstate New York home, we dined on her specialties: salt-fish for breakfast, plenty of meat (pork chops, ribs, steak, and chicken), greens, sweet potatoes, and coleslaw, a variety of soups, and cobblers and pies for dessert. Though we are each committed to different dietary choices, I savored the food she prepared and am grateful for the experience.

On the last night of the first week we met at the Summer Peacebuilding Institute in 2008, we enjoyed a potluck dinner. People from dozens of countries prepared meals from their different cultures that were shared with all. Sharon cooked a big pot of collard greens—an Ethiopian recipe—that she began preparing twenty-four hours in advance. She selected her ingredients carefully and described a ritual for cleaning the greens and spicing them just so. Well, that pot of greens barely saw the light of day. It was empty in five minutes. I was lucky to snag a small helping before they disappeared. Here I was in my fifties devouring this wonderful new food I can't recall having ever eaten before.

Sharon was shocked. "Greens are so much a part of what we eat. I am amazed at people who don't know what they are and how good they taste!"

Our entire journey together has been filled with such surprises. It begs the obvious. The way to break down barriers is get to know each other; spend time together. We'll find we have more in common than not—and that is a big first step. Such encounters—which I experience more now than ever before in my life—give me hope.

I recently found myself seated in the back row of a very full bus on my way across upstate New York to Sharon's house. An African American couple sat next to me. I was reading something in connection with systemic racism and I was pissed off. Not long ago, I would have sat there and stewed. Instead, I introduced myself to these complete strangers. It turned out they were social workers in New York City. We had a terrific discussion that made us wish we'd begun talking at the beginning of our ride rather than a few miles before it ended.

I think it's pretty amazing how far Sharon and I have come. After so much interaction, we're comfortable with each other. We've awakened in the same house and said good morning before wiping the sleep from our eyes. We've come to know each other's families and friends. But that's just us. What does it mean for others?

THE WAY FORWARD

It will be a great day indeed when people start listening to one another, looking truthfully at their ancestral experiences, recognizing the privilege that exists for white people and the horrible oppression that still takes place for people of color because of it.

In general, the big question is, how do we disentangle ourselves? How do we undo a racist justice system, a racist financial system, a racist healthcare system? They are all so deeply embedded in our society and in our individual lives. Most people understandably conclude that the problems are just too big. So we watch *The Real Housewives* or some such "reality" television program to escape from reality. That is not the answer. There *are* things we can do. We can't go back into history and correct the damage at its root, but we can learn from history, walk forward, and influence the future.

Many members of Coming to the Table exchange genealogical information. People of color are often stymied in their research because they can't find the records needed to confirm who they are and where they came from. That was one of the things that drew Sharon to Coming to the Table in the first place and is on her agenda for change. She wants to help people empower themselves through genealogy.

It would be invaluable to create a genealogy database that lists the name of every known enslaved person with links to documentation. Resources similar to the US Holocaust Memorial Museum in Washington, DC, with kiosks to plug in names of ancestors and find associated stories and images, would help. This would enable people to learn something about the culture and times in which their ancestors lived.

It is only when a critical mass of individuals begin to change that the opportunity arises for systemic, institutional reform. Individuals influence their communities; popular groundswell can lead to national dialogue. A starting point for thoughtful discussion about the legacy of slavery might be inspired by H.R. 40, the Commission to Study Reparation Proposals for African Americans Act, a bill sponsored by Representative John Conyers of Michigan, which has languished in Congress since it was first introduced in 1989. The bill would establish a commission to study slavery and subsequent racial and economic discrimination, and make recommendations on remedies to redress the harm. White people tend to recoil from Conyers's proposal because it speaks of "reparations." What is being overlooked is the more salient part; taking a truthful look at slavery and its legacy and considering repair in the light of restorative justice as opposed to getting stuck over the concept of financial remuneration.

The actions of one or two people rarely make a significant difference in the world. But the commitment of many people, acting individually and collectively, has great potential. Hope springs when people take the STAR training; when members of Coming to the Table congregate on a conference call to discuss restorative justice, genealogy, or relationship building; when six women in Seattle create a weekly "Healing Together" workshop; and when a man in Virginia inspires people in his community to explore the history and impact of slavery through Negro spirituals and to raise their voices together in song. Hope also bubbles when the owner of an antebellum home in Mississippi speaks frankly about the sins of the past, when Tom talks to the people next to him on the bus, and when Sharon delivers a pie to her neighbors.

This is our work: to repair unhealed wounds from the past and challenge systems that remain unjust and either dismantle them or work to make them just and repair the damage they continue to cause.

We would love to say of our experiment, "Boy, this is it! This is the lightning bolt! We've found *the* answer!" But it isn't that simple or tidy. We began as two disconnected people. We learned. We argued. We struggled. We grew. We laughed. We cried. We changed. Along the way, we became friends.

Our journey would not have had the same impact had we not traveled *together*; struggled and laughed and argued *together*; visited the graves, the courthouses, the museums, the places embodying both horror and hope . . . *together*. What we did was empowering. It brought history alive and into the present. We answered the call of our ancestors, confirming to ourselves how much they wanted us to find them so they could help us along. In the process, we learned new truths and gave our lizard brains a rest.

Ours is not the only way. Everyone needs to find their own path. Maybe it isn't two weeks in Tobago, a six-thousand-mile road trip, or a hundred thousand miles on jets (and way too large a carbon footprint). Whatever you choose to do, STAR and Coming to the Table can help you confront the issues and act on what you learn.

The lessons are in the quest. The answers are found in the journey. These are ripples on a pond. They spread outward.

And on we walk . . .

NOTES ON METHODOLOGY

"How on earth do I attempt to heal from such a huge traumatic wound as the one caused by the legacy of slavery and the racism it spawned?" That is the question we each asked ourselves long before we met. The answer we reached independently, that led to our meeting, the foundation for our journey, and this book is obvious now: start where you are.

We started in front of our computer screens. Coming to the Table entered our lives via e-mail and Internet links that drew us together in the same place at the same time: June 2008 at the Summer Peacebuilding Institute at Eastern Mennonite University in Harrisonburg, Virginia. Since then, we have doggedly pursued a deeper understanding of the wounds inflicted by racism through relationship building, research, and shared personal experience.

We both completed STAR (Strategies for Trauma Awareness & Resilience) training at EMU. That gave us a foundation for understanding trauma and its affects. We took what we learned and transformed it into a presentation module that we tested at the John Hope Franklin Reconciliation Conference in Tulsa, Oklahoma, and share with you to the best of our ability in these pages.

Between June 2008 and October 2011, we traveled more than one hundred thousand miles back and forth across the United States and overseas. The most significant single excursion, in spring 2011, was driving more than six thousand miles through twenty-one states in the Deep South, Midwest, and North. In total, we have visited twenty-seven states, the District of Columbia, and the island nation of Trinidad and Tobago.

The genealogical aspect of our research took us to courthouses in Illinois, Kentucky, Alabama, and Mississippi. We visited cemeteries in Illinois, Rhode Island, Kentucky, Alabama, Mississippi, Kansas, and California. Institutional research led us to museums, interpretive centers, and memorials in eleven states (Illinois, Washington, California, Rhode Island, Georgia, Alabama, Mississippi, Arkansas, Oklahoma, Ohio, and Virginia), and Washington, DC.

Among those that had the greatest impact were the Martin Luther King Jr. National Historic Site in Atlanta; the National Voting Rights Museum and the Selma-Montgomery Interpretive Center in and near Selma, Alabama; the Rosa Parks Museum at Troy University in Montgomery, Alabama; the Tuskegee Institute and George Washington Carver Museum in Tuskegee, Alabama; the John Hope Franklin Reconciliation Park in Tulsa; the Abraham Lincoln Presidential Library and Museum in Springfield, Illinois; the National Underground Railroad Freedom Center in Cincinnati; the Frontier Culture Museum in Staunton, Virginia; and Thomas Jefferson's Monticello in Charlottesville, Virginia.

Our research included evaluation of the STAR program, Coming to the Table (CTTT), and other models and assets. We interviewed many practitioners, including Elaine Zook Barge and Howard Zehr (in connection with their roles with the STAR and Restorative Justice programs at EMU); Jan Jenner, director of CTTT and the EMU Practice and Training Institute; Barbara "Sha" Jackson, associate director of CTTT; Susan Hutchison, community coordinator and cofounder of CTTT; and Phoebe Kilby, associate development director for the Center for Justice and Peacebuilding at EMU.

Among those in other leadership positions with CTTT, we interviewed Pat Russell, a teacher, family therapist, and community-based advocate in Seattle; Prinny Anderson, a consultant with Duke Corporate Education in Durham, North Carolina; Art Carter, a retired pediatrician and community activist on Virginia's Eastern Shore; David Pettee, director of ministerial credentialing with the Unitarian Universalist Association in Boston; and Will Hairston, cofounder of CTTT in Harrisonburg, Virginia.

We interviewed several people in connection with their leadership roles at interpretive museums, including Cheryl Taylor, executive director, Museum of the Mississippi Delta, Greenwood, Mississippi; Lucia C. Stanton, the Shannon Senior Research Historian with the Thomas Jefferson Foundation in Charlottesville, Virginia; and Georgette Norman, executive director of the Rosa Parks Library and Museum at Troy University in Montgomery, Alabama.

We also interviewed people working in the fields of racial justice and equity, including Sylvester "Tee" Turner, director of reconciliation programs at Hope in the Cities, in Richmond, Virginia; Vanessa Jackson, president of Healing Circles, Inc., in Atlanta; Mana Tahei, director of racial justice, YWCA; Kim Nave, chief operating officer, YWCA; and Felicia Collins Correia, chief executive officer, YWCA—all three from Tulsa, Oklahoma; and Donna Odom, executive director of the Southwest Michigan Black Heritage Society in Kalamazoo, Michigan.

We've done our best to reconstruct conversations to accurately reflect our experiences of them. Some names and details have been changed to protect the privacy of certain individuals. Our intention is to inform, not to vilify.

We devoured scores of books. The following were especially useful:

- Michelle Alexander. *The New Jim Crow: Mass Incarceration in the Age of Colorblindness.* New York: The New Press, 2010.
- Wendell Berry. *The Hidden Wound.* 1970. Reprint, San Francisco: North Point Press, 1989.
- Douglas A. Blackmon. *Slavery by Another Name: The Re-Enslavement of Black Americans from the Civil War to World War II.* New York: Doubleday, 2008.
- Roy L. Brooks. *Atonement and Forgiveness: A New Model for Black Reparations.* Berkeley: University of California Press, 2004.
- Joy DeGruy Leary. *Post Traumatic Slave Syndrome.* Milwaukie, OR: Uptone Press, 2005.
- Shelly Tochluk. *Witnessing Whiteness: The Need to Talk about Race and How to Do It.* Lanham, MD: Rowman & Littlefield Education, 2010.
- Carolyn Yoder. *The Little Book of Trauma Healing: When Violence*

Strikes and Community is Threatened. Intercourse, PA: Good Books, 2005.

- Howard Zehr. *The Little Book of Restorative Justice.* Intercourse, PA: Good Books, 2002.
- Howard Zinn. *A People's History of the United States.* New York: Harper, 2003.

Additional information and resources are available at the following websites: *STAR: Strategies for Trauma Awareness & Resilience* (www .emu.edu/star/), *Coming to the Table* (www.comingtothetable.org/), *Our Black Ancestry* (www.ourblackancestry.com/), *Inheriting the Trade* (http://inheritingthetrade.com/), and *Gather at the Table* (www.gather atthetable.net). We referred several times throughout this book to the "cycles of violence" as taught in the STAR training program at EMU. The Coming to the Table approach offers a path out of the cycles depicted in the "Cycles of Violence" illustration on the next page.

Cycles of Violence

TRAUMATIC EVENT(S) ACT(S) OF VIOLENCE

Physiological changes

Victim Cycle (Acting In)

Shock, injury, denial, anxiety, fear, depression

Realization of loss, panic

Suppression of grief and fears, numbing, isolation, silence

Anger, rage, spiritual questions, loss of meaning, self-abuse, addictions

Survivor guilt, shame and humiliation, internalized oppression

Learned helplessness, hopelessness, fatalism

Re-experiencing events, intrusive thoughts, avoiding reminders, hypervigilance

Fantasies of revenge, need for justice

Aggressor Cycle (Acting Out)

Attack in the name of self-defense, justice, or restoring honor

Social and cultural pressures, pride

Decision to pursue own needs, even at the expense of others

Seeing violence as redemptive

Dehumanization of the enemy

Development of good vs. evil narrative.

Unmet needs for safety and justice, shame, humiliation, fear

Seeing self/group as victims, increased group identity—"us vs. them"

Designed by Carolyn Yoder, STAR Program, 2004, revised November 2011. Copyright ©2011 Eastern Mennonite University. http://www.emu.edu/star.

ACKNOWLEDGMENTS

Our journey to *Gather at the Table* was enriched by the support, encouragement, and collaboration of many people who share our desire to make the world a better place by confronting the legacy of slavery and racism.

To the Center for Justice and Peacebuilding at Eastern Mennonite University, we are grateful for your commitment to Coming to the Table, the STAR program, and the Summer Peacebuilding Institute, all of which contribute in profound ways to teaching models of healing that are utilized throughout the world. Special kudos to Elaine Zook Barge, director of STAR, and Howard Zehr, professor of restorative justice. One-quarter of the royalties from *Gather at the Table* will be contributed to support the work of CTTT, STAR, and SPI.

We are deeply blessed to share the fellowship of our many friends in Coming to the Table. Your abiding commitment to truth, justice, mercy, and peace has been an inspiration every step of the way.

We salute the Fetzer Institute and W. K. Kellogg Foundation for their leadership in funding programs in racial equity and healing. Both provided significant financial support to Coming to the Table. Our work with WKKF was invaluable to the evolution of our thinking and our journey together.

Many individuals provided financial, lodging, and other forms of support to our project. Special thanks in this regard to Lita and Omowale

Richard Ahye, the Bennett family, Aldea and Lydia Coleman, Eugene and Renee Dixon, Lavona Goodson, Professor Hollis Lynch, Lawson and Beth Mabry, Helen Nadler, David Nicholson, Dain and Constance Perry, James DeWolf Perry, Belvie Rooks and Dedan Gills, Harold Rush, Brad and P.J. Sargeant, Sheryl Smith, and Dick Wing.

As we made our way around the United States, we were aided in our genealogical research by staff members at libraries, courthouses, and cemetery associations. We marvel at how generous they are with their time and expertise in helping those who wish to connect with ancestors.

Working with Beacon Press has been a delight. Your commitment to publishing books that enlighten people about peace, liberty, and justice for all is unsurpassed. We are forever grateful for your professionalism and support. We offer particular thanks to executive editor Gayatri Patnaik for your wisdom and partnership in the development of this book, and also to editorial assistant Rachael Marks and copy editor Monica Jainschigg. Beacon's director, Helene Atwan; director of sales and marketing, Tom Hallock; communications director, Pamela MacColl; and publicist, Reshma Melwani, have been invaluable allies.

We extend our deep gratitude to Joy DeGruy. Your work inspires us and permeates these pages.

Finally, our profound gratitude to our families; your love and support helps keep us on track in all our endeavors. From Tom: Thanks to my children, Shiloh, Emily, Russell, and Jolie, for invigorating my life; and to my grandchildren, Seth, Alison, George, James, Olive, Gracie, and Mariana, for all your kisses and smiles. To my wife, Lindi, thank you for sharing this lifetime with me, for your patience, and for joining Sharon and me from time to time in the warm places. From Sharon: Thanks to my Uncle Irving and Aunt June Nicholson for lifelong support and allowing us the solace and inspiration of the Three Rivers house. Special thanks to my son, Vincent, and his wife, Shola, both of whom are committed to public service and educating people about the challenging issues of today. To my grandchildren, Julian and Violet, your warm little hugs are more than an inspiration. We love you all. Thank you from the bottom of our hearts for walking with us on this journey.

NOTES

CHAPTER ONE: THE RECALCITRANT BAT

1. "Population of T & T at Census Dates: 1960–2000," *Trinidad & Tobago Today*, http://www.cso.gov.tt/.

CHAPTER TWO: CASTAWAYS FROM SECURITY ISLAND

1. Mennonite Church History, http://history.mennonite.net/; "Opportunities and Challenges: Racial/Ethnic Mennonites in the United States," *Mennonite Magazine*, February 6, 2007, 15, http://www.themennonite.org/.

CHAPTER FOUR: LIZARD BRAIN

1. Jason Marsh et al., *Are We Born Racist?* (Boston: Beacon Press, 2010), 4.
2. John Cloud, "Why Your DNA Isn't Your Destiny," *Time*, January 6, 2010, http://www.time.com/.

CHAPTER FIVE: MANY RIVERS TO CROSS

1. 1927 Chicago Municipal Code, "Jim Crow Laws: Illinois," *The History of Jim Crow*, http://jimcrowhistory.org/.
2. Schomburg Center for Research in Black Culture; *In Motion: The African-American Migration Experience*, http://www.inmotionaame.org/.

CHAPTER SIX: THE PAST IS PRESENT

1. "Crafting the Oregon Constitution," http://arcweb.sos.state.or.us/.

2. James W. Loewen, *Sundown Towns* (New York: New Press, 2005), 410.

3. "Portland Neighborhoods, 1960s–Present: Race and Progressive Resistance," Oregon History Project, http://www.ohs.org/.

4. National Archives and Records Administration, Dawes Commission Case File #MCR 2209, transcript of testimony of Bettie Gavin, May 15, 1901.

CHAPTER SEVEN: COLORED WATER

1. New Orleans lynching: "Dark Legacy," David Pacchioli, Pennsylvania State University online research, http://www.rps.psu.edu/; Edward F. Haas, "Guns, Goats, and Italians: The Tallulah Lynching of 1899," *North Louisiana Historical Association* XIII, nos. 2/3, 1982, http://www.rootsweb.ancestry.com/; "The Story of Italian American Internment during WWII"; Italian Historical Society of America, http://www.italianhistorical.org/.

2. Celia McGee, "The Open Road Wasn't Quite Open to All," *New York Times*, August 22, 2010, http://www.nytimes.com/.

CHAPTER EIGHT: CYCLES OF VIOLENCE

1. Drew Griffin and Scott Bronstein, "Video Shows White Teens Driving Over, Killing Black Man, Says DA," CNN Special Investigations, August 8, 2011, http://www.cnn.com/.

2. Drew Griffin and Scott Bronstein, "Family of Alleged Hate-Killing Victim Opposes Death Penalty in Case," CNN Special Investigations Unit, September 14, 2011 http://articles.cnn.com/.

3. "Lynchings: By State and Race, 1882–1968," University of Missouri-Kansas City School of Law, statistics provided by the Archives at Tuskegee Institute, http://law2.umkc.edu/.

4. "Two Accuse Policemen of Serious Assault," *Star (South Africa)*, November 6, 1995.

5. "American Brutalised by Policeman Vindicated," SAPA News Wire (South Africa), December 20, 1996.

CHAPTER NINE: GRAVE MATTERS

1. Boyce Watkins, "Famous Doctor Operated on Slaves Without Anesthesia," *Huffington Post*, December 10, 2010, http://www.bvblackspin.com/.

CHAPTER TEN: THE CROSSROADS OF LIBERTY AND COMMERCE

1. "The Neo-Confederates," *Intelligence Report,* no. 99 (Summer 2000), Southern Poverty Law Center, http://www.splcenter.org/.

CHAPTER ELEVEN: TRUTH BE TOLD

1. Robert A. Gibson, "The Negro Holocaust: Lynching and Race Riots in the United States, 1880–1950," Yale-New Haven Teachers Institute, http://yale.edu/ynhti/.

CHAPTER THIRTEEN: RIPPLES ON A POND

1. Philip J. Mazzocco et al., "The Cost of Being Black: White Americans' Perceptions and the Question of Reparations," *Du Bois Review* 3 (2006): 261–97.